Your Ha

MW00440759

Su Mano en Mi Mano

The Memoirs of a Former Peace Corps Volunteer

Tim Flaherty

ISBN:1469957094
ISBN-13: 978-1469957098

DEDICATION

This book is dedicated to my mom and dad and my
brother, Todd, all of whom I'd give anything to
have back with me right now. This memoir is for
all my family, especially my children Vicky and
Santy and my grandson, Brady.

This book is also dedicated to a lasting peace and
democracy for all the people of Guatemala.

CONTENTS

ACKNOWLEDGMENTS

First of all I must acknowledge the help I found in one very special book. The name of that book is "The Area Handbook for Guatemala." This edition was printed in March of 1970. This volume is one of a series of handbooks prepared by Foreign Area Studies of The American University. This book was invaluable as it clearly defined the culture and the many customs of the people of Guatemala. If one wants to learn and understand the beautiful Mayan nation, then this book is a must read. This manuscript reveals to the reader all aspects of the land of Guatemala, complete with the religious, cultural and political energy and soul. Before all the politics of Guatemala, there was humanity.

Another book that I purchased was "Bitter Fruit," which was written in 1982 by Stephen Schlesinger who is the Director of the World Policy Institute. His co-author is Stephen Kinzer, cultural correspondent for The New York Times. This book is considered a classic, as it tells of the American CIA's involvement in overthrowing the democratically elected government of President Jacobo Arbenz in 1954. This book reveals how the power of the United States can sometimes be dangerous and abusive.

The third source of acknowledgement is "The Life World Library on Central America." This book was written by Harold Lavine and The Editors of Life Magazine. This book displays some very outstanding photos of the Guatemalan lifestyle. From this book, the reader learns of the landless poor, the democrats and the dictators and the work that lies ahead toward tomorrow. The photos are tremendous and truthful in content and color, simply breathtaking.

My editor for *Su Mano en Mi Mano,* Your Hand in My Hand, is Mr. Harrison Beck who is presently studying playwriting and dramatic arts at The New York University in Manhattan, New York. Harrison devoted his time and energy toward the success of this story. The formatting and other technical aspects of self-publishing this book was done by Ms. Pamela Jones. The beautiful cover art was produced by Ms. Elizabeth Diccico.

PART ONE

This story is my reminiscence of a time in life when a young person boasted about what he thought was immortality. Could we live forever? Would we refuse to die? Could scientists isolate the aging gene and eliminate it from our genetic makeup? Those were sentiments back in the late 20th century. In 1979 I was going back to Guatemala, "Land of the Eternal Spring." I devoted my Peace Corps experience to serving in Guatemala, a nation of 3 million people, from June of 1974 until the end of December of 1976. This was a land whose people would profoundly change a person's life and infuse the feeling of invincibility. And a Peace Corps Volunteer could be ripe for the taking. With all the experience of getting to know Guatemala, I was confident that I could bring my step-son, Santos Ramirez, also known to all as

Santy, back to America. He is the main focus of this story along with the treacherous journey of taking him to the United States. I met Santy's mother, Miriam, while serving in Guatemala and we were married in January of 1977. She is a very courageous woman from Guatemala. But this trip wasn't a sentimental voyage where Santy and I would luckily return to Miami and then on to Boston. This adventure ended up being an extremely difficult task undertaken by one individual. What took place was perhaps close to being nearly impossible. There was one challenge met by another even harder confrontation. Every struggle and accomplishment were fought for and pushed to the limit.

I must acknowledge that in 1979 while in Guatemala City, during this mission, I was lucky enough to be able to stay at the home of a young former student, Veronica Rivera. I met Veronica in 1978 while working as a Spanish speaking job counselor at Keefe Technical High School in Framingham, Massachusetts. I knew her older sister who offered to let me stay at her parent's home in the capital, Guatemala City. Without their support my trip would have been even more difficult than it was.

Americans used to characterize and call the Central American countries banana republics.

There in lies their curse, for the poor of that region have been mostly taken advantage of and stripped of their identity. And with that kind of loss, one is only left with the image of corrupt government officials exploiting the poor and indigent population of Guatemala. These countries were not taken seriously until Cuba turned Communist in the late 1950's. Due to a close geographic proximity to Cuba, the Central American nations then became strategically important to the United States. That's precisely what the United States wanted all along. The Central American countries were at the beck and call of the ultimate neighbor north of the Rio Grande, the United States of America. Remarkably enough, when speaking about bananas, Guatemala and Honduras could rightly boast that they were the only two countries in the region that could initially grow bananas back in the early 20th century. Ultimately though, bananas were grown successfully throughout much of Latin America. The climate was perfect for this fruit that originally came from the South Seas beyond Hawaii. What became relevant and important was the fact that The United Fruit Company of the USA helped export the bananas from Guatemala and made a great profit doing so. In that respect, the United Fruit Company took the very best of what these countries had to offer in terms of their natural resources. One could easily compare this to the tremendous amounts of gold the conquistadores four centuries earlier took back to Spain and Portugal. In the 1950's the Guatemalan agricultural laborers earned very little for their work, wages barely enough to live on. That is fact and Americans should be aware of this history.

In essence, this anthem is in some measure about two countries that stood side by side down below Mexico. Politically, Guatemala simmered while at times El Salvador was brutally hot and tortured. To serve and live as a Peace Corps volunteer in either of these two countries was to have a front row seat at how republics function under military dictatorships. American Peace Corps volunteers were not allowed to partake or demonstrate against that corrupt political system. Therefore one could only be outspoken, yet reserved in opinion for one's preservation. This edict made one feel like a boxer who has to fight with one hand tied behind his back. The director of Peace Corps operations in Guatemala warned all new volunteers not to get politically involved. If one did, then he'd be sent back to Washington DC for early termination.

The power in Guatemala was distributed at the top of the government. All those quasi- military types had their hands reaching out for payoffs. Life went on regardless of what your politics were. That's how the rest of the population pushed ahead and retained civility. The poor were interested in how they would support and feed a family. Politics were beyond them and political progress was hopeless for the lower class. With great frustration, it was perceived by many that a better life did not exist in Guatemala but in possibly going to the United States in search of work. With a secure job, a man or woman could send money home to their families. In Santy's case, his mother, Miriam, went alone to Los Angeles, California in order to work as a domestic. She entrusted her earnings to a dishonest woman who Miriam thought was her friend. This woman took the cash Miriam gave her, and kept it for herself rather than mailing it to Miriam's mother in Guatemala. Miriam didn't realize any of this until after we were married in January of 1977. Miriam's mother, back in Guatemala, never received any of the money. Her mother, Doña Victoria, also didn't have any contact with Miriam until after she moved to Massachusetts. A crooked friend's betrayal of this nature could sometimes happen frequently to those who were unaware.

Therefore I have come to recognize all of these images of lives, countries and personal accomplishments as streams converging and joining a great river. These were human resources that were all meeting at the same delta, pouring all that they had into one giant reserve of energy. These resources all drained into the sea and universe. All the people in this narrative either directly related to Santy or otherwise, sacrificed their time for the same purpose. My friends in Guatemala are very important to me and will always remain so, as we continue to be up to the present. I went to their country to lend my expertise in the field of agriculture, specifically animal husbandry. In turn, Guatemalans taught me invaluable lessons in life that have been set forth in this story. From this global perspective, nature is waiting to reveal itself via human triumph. On the cosmic level, we became aware of a force from beyond the stars in the heavens, and from the guiding hands of eternity. Therefore, let this river flow and change the bravado into bravura and acknowledge perhaps the presence, power and passion of a divine intervention.

Let this account stand as a memoir not just of the main figures whose lives have been forever changed by their experience, but of many others who have collectively put the Central American world atop their shoulders for the advancement of humanity. The Mayans are a great and strong people with the banner of the sun. Perhaps they are destined to be the masters of time, conceivably the closest to their God. Guatemala will stand with head held high despite the present civil strife, as well as its violent and turbulent past. They must deal with the damage to their nation's image. But they don't want to be endlessly defined by it. This land and people have contributed in the making of this tale while continuing to work for freedom, equality, a lasting peace and democracy.

It was 1979 and my wife Miriam, now wanted to bring her seven year old son, Santy to the United States. However, Santy was living with his grandmother in Guatemala City, the capital of Guatemala in Central America. Santy's grandmother, Doña Victoria, loved him very dearly and treated him just like a son. In turn, Santy adored and loved her as his mother, as she was practically the only maternal figure he knew. Due to these circumstances, Doña Victoria wasn't very enthusiastic about letting Santy go to the states. In Guatemala the family was sacred and came first above all. I knew all this, well before I decided to go on the trip. I was the one who had to go to Guatemala because Santy's mom, was still just a legal resident and not yet a US citizen. If she went to Guatemala, she may have been detained and unable to get Santy out of the country, spending time and money needlessly. And due to Miriam's strong emotional bond with her mother, she may have relented and given in to her and allowed Santy to remain in Guatemala.

It was now the fall season in New England, October of 1979, with each day growing in anticipation, and I had to buy my plane ticket. A friend of mine who worked for a travel agency was able to get me a round trip ticket on United Airlines. The cost was only three hundred and fifty dollars with the stipulation I go and return within one month. If my stay was longer, I would have to pay an extra hundred and fifty dollars. This was reasonable and I figured that the trip wouldn't take more than thirty days. I also managed to take another five hundred dollars with me, mostly in traveler's checks. This seemed like enough money. I told my wife Miriam, Santy's mom, not to worry and that I was sure and confident I could bring Santy back with me.

After saying goodbye to my mom and dad, I reassured Miriam I'd return with Santy. After saying my goodbyes, both my wife Miriam and my brother Dennis drove me to Logan Airport and to the United Airlines terminal. Dennis wished me good luck and we shook hands and said goodbye, while I then gave Miriam a big hug and kiss to help calm her. In 1979 Logan Airport was small compared to the near, state-of-the- art metropolis it is today. There was no threat of terrorist attack and security was barely a presence. Eastern Airlines was still in business and their terminal was on the right as one drove into the airport. Dividing the airport down the middle was a parking lot where travelers could safely leave their cars behind if needed.

My flight was an early one, and the plane took off at 8:00 am and had only a two hour stop in Miami Airport. The flight seemed routine as we flew off the eastern coast while any passengers who were interested could look out their windows at some fishing boats working off the shore of Georgia. The visibility was nearly perfect on that chilly early October day.

Without any flight problems, we arrived in Miami at about twelve noon. The airport seemed like it was at the crossroads of civilization with many people coming and going, confident as to where they were headed. Miami Airport was much bigger than Logan and most of the small stores had many employees who could only speak in English. Likewise, some of the Spanish people working behind the counter at the soda fountain casually assumed me to be Hispanic and asked me in Spanish what I wanted. As there were many people from all over Latin America, I enjoyed speaking with Spanish customers helping some of the store employees who couldn't speak their language. Miami was host to many Cubans as well as many from other parts of the Caribbean.

I had a quick lunch of fruit salad with yogurt, along with a glass of mango juice. When I finished eating I went to the Guatemalan airlines, the Aviateca terminal at 2:00 pm where I boarded a plane as nice as the one from United. We were bound for Guatemala and found ourselves over the Caribbean at about five miles up. Time seemed to flow by just as effortlessly as the clouds passing my window. Before I knew it, there was a festive array of vibrant shades of green colors glowing in front of my eyes as we flew over Guatemala.

Aside from the fantastic flora of green jungle foliage, I could readily see the radiant Lake Atitlan from high above. There was a saying in Guatemala that Lake Atitlan was the *espejo del cielo* or in English "mirror of heaven," and from every vantage point Lake Atitlan was a striking and crystal clear blue, reflecting the sky and heavens from high above. Whether from near or far, it stood out so prominently, radiating from high above, the heat of the sun, dashing about and within like a vial of quick silver. On one weekend during my Peace Corps service, I traveled to see Lake Atitlan. I was taken out onto the lake in a large rowboat by a man who was Mayan Indian. He and his family lived in the village of Sololá, near the shoreline. He showed me first- hand how clear and blue the water was while guiding and pushing the boat along in the water with a long pole. I was very impressed at how the Mayans kept the lake from being polluted. The Mayans were very neat and clean, always keeping their clothing fresh and nearly spotless as well. It was very common to see Mayan women washing their family's clothes with a bar of laundry soap on the large rocks of the water's edge.

After being out on the lake, my guide had invited me up and into the small and intimate house that he had made from adobe. He introduced me to his wife and children and showed me the tomb site of one of his children who died at birth. The burial place of the infant was eight feet down in the earth in what above was their living room. It seemed fitting that one would bury their child that way. There was a sense of sacred beauty and holiness in the love that this man had for his family. Such devotion was perhaps why the Mayan people who lived in this small village kept the land and water looking serene, reflecting their purity and goodness. And that's why the lake caught my eye so quickly from a few miles above.

As the plane approached Guatemala's Aurora International Airport, my anticipation grew. There is something very special about Guatemala. The one word to describe this is *ambiente,* the ambience, where life and the atmosphere have a slower pace and people take time to enjoy living with lightheartedness. Within just a few days one will notice the great appeal of their culture and customs, leaving one with a wonderful impression. The sights and sounds of Guatemala are pleasantly intoxicating with a sensation that's both healing and bonding.

As the plane touched down without any problems at all, I entered the terminal and looked for the members of the Rivera family who I knew in Guatemala City. Finally, I saw the student I was looking for, Veronica Rivera. One of the first jobs I had after returning home to Massachusetts from my Peace Corps service was as a Spanish speaking job developer. I was hired in September 1977 at Keefe Technical High School in Framingham, Massachusetts, a city with a large Spanish population. One of my tasks included teaching English as a second language. Veronica, a young and vibrant teenager with a quick and ready smile, was one of my students before she returned to her native Guatemala after living for a year in Framingham with family relatives. After getting to know her aunt and uncle in the Framingham community, I was invited to stay at her mother's home at Zone 3, in Guatemala City. The capital of Guatemala is subdivided into sectors, or what they refer to as Zones designed by urban engineering. There are 22 Zones in all. Each one has its own streets and avenues, making it very easy to find addresses in the city. With Zones, the Guatemalan people were able to simplify their movement and ability to reach anyone they wanted to see, via a sometimes easy and adventurous, but hot and dusty bus ride through their capital city.

Pleasantly, Veronica was a bright, intelligent student, and she had quickly learned English in the time she lived in the states. But she preferred to speak in Spanish and I had no problem speaking the same. As they lived close to the United States Embassy, staying with the Rivera family made it easier for me while I went to that district each day. This was all pre-arranged before I left on the trip. I didn't have the added expense of a hotel room, nor did I want to burden Doña Victoria by staying at her home.

At Veronica's home, I was taken to a very clean and comfortable room on the second floor. After unpacking my suitcase, I walked out on to the second floor balcony and saw that the house had a high cement wall of cinder-block built around it. At the very top of the wall were many small pieces of broken jagged glass. This element gave their home an even greater protection from any outsiders, such as thieves who were adept at breaking and entering any home with the intention of robbing and stealing. After going back down stairs to the living room, I asked Veronica where the US Embassy was located. She said it was close by in Zone 10.

I liked a challenge and was enthusiastic with the task of bringing Santy to the states, despite all the possible red tape that awaited me. The first thing I did after settling into Veronica's home was to sit down and have dinner with her family. Veronica's grandmother Doña Louisa as well as her mother Teco conveyed a serenity and kindness. Teco was a graphic designer and her sister, Veronica's aunt, Myra was a school teacher while her husband Rudolfo worked as a mechanical engineer. We all ate baked chicken with salad, rice and black beans with tortillas. All of these foods were in abundance here in the capital. The beverage at supper was a cup of tea or black coffee, as was custom in Guatemala. I had not enjoyed Guatemalan style food for two years. The food this family served was a welcome change, and it all made me feel sentimental about my past Peace Corps service in Guatemala. I remembered that it had taken me about two or three months to get used to eating tortillas and black beans. Sometimes, depending on where one ate, either bread or tortillas were provided. But to watch a woman make a tortilla was like seeing how my mother would shape a hamburger before placing the food on the grill. The main ingredient of the tortilla was fresh corn that had been soaked in water and then drained. The corn was ground from the indispensable, *metate,* the two hand held stones used for grinding the corn by hand into a pliable dough. The tortilla is then made from the corn flour that is shaped and flattened like a pancake. While shaping the tortilla, it sounds as if the woman is clapping her hands in appreciation. The tortilla is then placed on the flat hot surface of a griddle and cooked over a wood fire. Just the aroma of the wood burning conjured up visions of the savory taste of this food considered, *típica,* distinctive cooking of Guatemala. Another change also included eating eggs in not only the morning but also in the evening as well. If one didn't want eggs that frequently, all they had to do was simply tell the host. Chicken, called *pollo* in Spanish, was sold everywhere in Guatemala. Chicken livers and gizzards were sold in bulk and even the chicken's claw was used to add flavor to a soup or broth. Chicken was so abundant that at least two restaurant chains, Pollo Campero and Los Pollos, were very popular, especially in Guatemala City. In fact chicken was so renowned, there was even a song written in its honor. That song was called *Que Le Mate el Pollo,* and when translated meant "Kill the Chicken." The song was first played in 1974 and was very popular for about two years on Guatemalan radio every day.

One particular product that I ate on a daily basis while I was in the Peace Corps was the food called Incaparina, an oatmeal cereal served hot. In 1959 the Institute of Nutrition of Central America and Panama, INCAP, located in Guatemala City, developed this low cost dietary supplement in order to combat malnutrition. Incaparina, named after the founding group INCAP, was made from cottonseed meal, corn, sorghum, calcium carbonate, yeast, and vitamin A. All of these ingredients were locally available foods which were ground to the consistency of flour. The mixture was equal to fresh milk in protein and vitamin A content. All it took was hot water or milk and a little bit of sugar to prepare Incaparina. It was developed so that any and all Guatemalan children would receive proper nourishment. Whenever I had to have a quick breakfast, I'd prepare a warm bowl of Incaparina with milk and a banana.

After finishing and thanking the family for dinner I wanted to take a walk into Veronica's neighborhood. As the weather was so pleasant and it was still the early evening, many people were out for a leisurely walk, running an errand, or talking with neighbors while children played by their side. The small corner stores were busy and would stay open until about nine at night. I wanted to look for a small bar where I could relax with a beer. I knew there was a cantina about three blocks away from Veronica's home. Upon reaching it, I entered the establishment and was welcomed. I was an American but Guatemalans welcomed any *gringos* who were just passing through. After all, they never wanted to let a "green go," meaning the green money that could be made. First, I went to the bar and asked the bar tender for *un Gallo,* the popular brand name beer sold throughout Guatemala. I paid for the beer and then went to sit at a table. From my table I could peacefully sit and listen to marimba, the music of Guatemala and ranchero style, music of Mexico. After just about ten minutes, a goon squad of plainclothes government forces suddenly entered the cantina with heavy duty artillery. I quickly sat up in my chair and started to feel very uncomfortable. I didn't know why they were there. At last one of them looked at me and assured me in Spanish that I was "even safer now than before." He further told me that they were looking for what was considered to be guerrilla activity. This was reassuring, but I wasn't at all comfortable around the danger of a shootout. Some of the men were carrying machine guns with large rolls of bullets wrapped and slung from around their shoulders. The government forces held their weapons high and very securely in their hands. It was almost as if the men were caressing the barrels of those powerful deadly weapons, slowly and methodically stroking them. Brazen in manner, they flaunted those guns up and down, embracing them with foul, greasy, oily hands. As if in a trance, the plainclothesmen had a menacing look, with stinging, piercing eyes that seemed as though they could have burned holes through any bystander. These hunters were in a state of euphoria, as if they couldn't wait to shoot somebody, anybody, just as long as they could satisfy what appeared to be their hunger for violence. A few of them were armed with powerful handguns that were drawn, locked and loaded. Not to be denied were those remaining, who carried sawed off shotguns, M-16's and machetes. Strangely enough all of these thugs were really little men with big guns. This was the decadence of guerrilla warfare. This scene was the last thing I ever wanted to see. These men were dressed in ordinary street cloths and looked like they could fit into any environment. Some of them had on cowboy hats, and reminded me of the men who were from Asuncion Mita, the town where I served and resided, in the county of Jutiapa. Feeling very uneasy, I finished my beer, got up and left the cantina in a hurry. I thought I'd escaped a close call and felt lucky to be leaving without any further difficulty. I reached Veronica's home and entered without telling the family what had just occurred. Although they were concerned for my safety, they would have told me that what happened was considered the lifestyle of their country. Their proverb was people should anticipate the unexpected. As the evening was drawing to a close, I said good night to Veronica's family and went to my room. There was plenty of work ahead, and the first thing I had to do in the morning was go and see Doña Victoria and young Santy, now seven years old, who I had not seen in nearly three years. His grandmother knew I was coming to Guatemala and expected me to arrive at her home at any time. My mother in law, Doña Victoria couldn't come to the airport as she didn't have any means of transportation. That was all fine as I planned to see her and the family very soon after I landed. I would have called by phone, only like many Guatemalan families, Veronica's family didn't have one in the home. Nor did Doña Victoria.

After a good night's sleep, I woke up to a beautiful sunny October day, without the brisk feeling of an autumnal chill or wind. There were no red, yellow or orange leaves falling to the ground. In fact there were few such trees in Guatemala. There were mostly tall striking and inviting palm or coconut trees.

October may have been autumn in the states, but it marked the end of the rainy season in Guatemala. When the rains come in Central America, it's a torrential downpour all day long. All the rain is a welcome sight for the farmers because it helps the *milpa,* their plot of fertile land to grow corn, black beans, soy beans and other crops. Some farmers were so jubilant and thankful for the rain that they would often wade knee high through the water in the early morning, with a *gracias a Dios para la luvia,* thanking God for the blessing of their crops. If one was careless and didn't wear a rain poncho, they might catch a bad chest cold lasting the three months of the rainy season. This was especially bad for the Mayan Indian population because very often they didn't have the money to see a doctor. However, a good pharmacist could recommend an over the counter medication for bronchitis. Other medicine such as penicillin or any other antibiotic could be sold without a written prescription. These drugs were made available because many Guatemalans didn't have sufficient money for a doctor's visit. For many people in Guatemala, especially Mayan Indians who lived in the mountainous lake regions, the flu virus could last indefinitely, perhaps lasting for months. If left untreated, one could possibly develop asthma or pneumonia. Without proper medical treatment, children and elderly patients especially the Mayan population, were at the highest risk for this illness. It was especially disheartening to see a young Mayan woman holding her baby in her arms while telling me *No hay remedio para gripa,* there's no cure for a bad cold. Fortunately, we were all in luck because when I arrived in Guatemala the rains had stopped and the weather was very comfortable and a warm eighty degrees with the sun out every day.

SU MANO EN MI MANO

I quickly showered and dressed so I could start the process of getting Santy a visa at the US Embassy. I had to go to Zone 7, where seven year old Santy lived with his grandmother, Tia Marta, Santy's aunt, a single parent who helped her mother with cleaning and laundry. To round out this cheerful tranquil home was Uncle Oscar, a hustling, hardworking, chain smoking young man who put his family first. These were my in-laws, as well as Santy's little, precious toddler cousin, Juan Pablo, Tia Marta's son.

When I got to their home I was welcomed with a strong maternal embrace from Doña Victoria and the entire family. Doña Victoria had a look of melancholy perhaps brought on by Santy's imminent departure. Doña Victoria was a very empathic, beautiful and soulful woman, almost saint like. She never raised her voice or her hand. She was very religious, Evangelical, and at complete peace with the world around her. Doña Victoria and her family were humble, and lived by modest means. Her family was able to combine their resources, including the help that her daughter, Miriam was able to send every month. Santy was only seven years old and he approached me slowly and didn't recognize me at all. I hugged him and gave him a kiss on the cheek and he returned the same. Santy looked a bit tired and underweight. His interaction was a little slow but I attributed that to his being shy. I also had to take into consideration that he had a hernia operation just about two years earlier. Santy had suffered with this hernia for a number of years before having the matter surgically corrected.

I explained to Doña Victoria, Marta and Oscar my plan to bring Santy to the states and they seemed in accord with everything, especially that Santy's mother, Miriam wanted to be reunited with him and for Santy to live in the United States. All seemed fine, as I presented my sister in law, Marta with a little suit that Miriam bought for Juan Pablo. Marta had him try it on and it was a perfect fit, just as if she took the child's suit off the rack at Bloomingdales. Oscar was about to leave for his work at a sugar cane plant and he left to catch a bus. I politely asked Santy's grandmother, Doña Victoria, if I could take Santy to lunch. We would then go to the US Embassy to start completing the paperwork. She agreed and with that Santy and I left the home and caught the bus that would make the stop at the Embassy.

In 1979 the buses were public transportation and still the only way many Guatemalan people without cars were able to trek and move around in the capital. We seemed to be in the hustle and bustle of the city with people crammed in and many passengers standing when there were no seats left. The buses, strictly "local," would sometimes make numerous stops to let people off and on. If one were to get off the bus in a busy part of the city, they would often be able to eat a quick lunch or supper. There would be *salchichas,* franks served at hot dog stands or the popular favorite, *tortilla con chicharone.* This light meal featured a tortilla filled with small pieces of pork baked inside the corn flour. On top of the flat tortilla with pork would be a topping of seasoned coleslaw. The combination would only cost twenty five *centavitos,* cents. Other means of public transportation included the taxis in the *Parke Central,* all parked next to what was the Guatemalan president's palace and residence. The cost of taking a taxi could end up being expensive if one didn't know how to bargain with the taxi drivers, as there was no set fee. And if the customer didn't realize all this, then he was really taken for the "wrong" kind of ride. Much to the owner's credit, most all the cars they had were vintage American made vehicles that were well kept and maintained.

I scanned the bus and saw a cross section of the Guatemalan people with many going to work or merely getting from one part of the city to another, perhaps reaching out to their families. Whether one was rich or poor, the family circle was the most important union for the people. In Guatemala, a son or daughter could live indefinitely with his or her parents. If married, they could live in the family home for as long as necessary with this custom an inherent part of the culture. If the adult children happened to live near their parents, they would find a way and reason to visit them nearly every day. Their family devotion was admirable and impressive as Guatemalan family bonds were very strong.

In just ten minutes, the bus stopped outside of the US Embassy and in clear view stood a line of Guatemalan people that practically stretched around the whole city block. I didn't realize it until I was told that if one was American, he could go directly to the front of the line.

As soon as I knew this, Santy and I worked our way to the front where we entered the Embassy. We went to the front desk and were attended to by a pleasant Guatemalan woman who spoke Spanish. I told her I wanted to fill out papers for my stepson, Santy, more formerly known on his birth certificate as Santos Ulysses Ramirez. I showed the woman the birth certificate from Santy's mother stating that Santy was born in Santana, El Salvador. She then asked me where Santy was residing and I told her that he was living with his grandmother in Zone 7. Her questions were very formal as she asked me if he had a passport and I stated he didn't. I was about to find out a very shocking surprise. Santy had been living in Guatemala in principle, illegally for the past seven years of his life. The lady informed me that I would have to take Santy to the city of Santana down in El Salvador in order to apply for his visa that would indicate his citizenship and when he left that country. This was the law and there was nothing I could do about it. I was nearly overwhelmed at hearing this setback. I had never planned to go to El Salvador. A trip to Salvador would have been extremely perilous, especially with a young child along side. I already knew that my Guatemala was unstable enough as it was, but holding together and for the time being safe enough for Americans.

I was absolutely bewildered and felt blind sided by the Embassy woman's last words. I felt as though I had just been punched in the stomach and lost all my wind and breath. Why didn't Santy's mother realize any of this before I went on this mission? Obviously she didn't know that there was a one dollar daily fine assessed to anyone who lived in Guatemala without a visa and passport. I was upset and angry but realized the complexity of the situation. The only way I could stay calm was to meditate and find consolation in talking about the dilemma with my friends. That was advice that would all come later when I spoke to Teco, Veronica's mother. Teco was street wise and knew the workings of her government and the politics that simmered, sometimes unfairly. She was a student out of the school of hard knocks. Teco was to later become the architect of nearly all my action taken from that day on. Thus, she lived up to her saying, "behind every successful man is a great woman."

At no time did I fill out any paperwork, so at least in retrospect I wasn't leaving any paper trail. The whole procedure sounded unreasonable and entailed a lot of red tape, but it seemed as though I had no other choice. I was crestfallen and felt as though I had a war going on in my head. But I knew I had to maintain a persona. Santy was too young to understand fully what was going on and it was just as well. In disbelief, I then thanked the woman and we left the Embassy. I began to remember the times when I went to the city of Santana to buy supplies for my different projects. Santana was a large city in El Salvador near the south eastern border of Guatemala, yet still about a half hour drive in *la camioneta,* an old rickety, run down bus that traveled everyday of the week from Santana and the Guatemalan border. Santy had lived all seven years of his life with the exception of the first week where his mother gave birth to him in Santana. While crossing the border of El Salvador and Guatemala, Miriam never took out any registration papers for him. Salvadorian army soldiers were ordered stationed and on duty at the border and they were casual and care-free, complacent and receptive to conversation. They were large, peaceful, mostly corpulent younger career soldiers with cheerful dispositions, just as long as one was sincere and honest. People were allowed to come and go as they pleased, just as long as they didn't look suspicious and had their passports. Little infants and children never drew any attention in that era. Nevertheless, the lack of validation could eventually arise as problematic while attempting to take Santy to America.

Without documentation, Santy was a non resident, and therefore considered illegal in Guatemala. Guatemalan immigration charges one dollar a day as a penalty and fine for not having proper residency papers. As this story evolved in reoccurring themes, Santy's birth certificate would become a major issue, a nearly insurmountable crisis to overcome. For now as it was only the middle of the afternoon, I decided to slow the pace down and take Santy to lunch. Even though I was still somewhat reeling in a state of uncertainty, I thought that breaking for lunch would allow me to reflect on what happened at the Embassy.

I had an American friend in Guatemala City who married a woman from Guatemala. They met while at college in New England. This young man was to become indispensible during my quest. His name was Danny Capone and he opened an Italian restaurant located on the Fifth Avenue near the

Central Park and presidential palace. As he and his wife, Rosa, named their first baby daughter "Amichi" they decided on naming the restaurant "Amichi Capone." It was such a darling and lovely name. Danny and his wife Rosa, a woman with a natural timeless beauty, ran the restaurant with the help of his in-laws in Guatemala City. The restaurant was very successful and I wanted very much to take Santy there for his very first pizza. After we were seated, Danny came out to the dining room as soon as Santy and I arrived and welcomed us. I stood to greet him with a hand shake. He was happy to see us and I introduced Santy to him. Danny was a bright and handsome young man who always had a warm smile on his face. We were seated at one of the tables and given menus. After I explained to Santy what a pizza was we decided to order one, along with two orange sodas. I had the feeling that he would like pizza. When the food arrived, I cut a couple of slices for Santy and he seemed to really like the new food. He ate his two slices and wanted more. Santy ate as much as he wanted as he suddenly showed me a good appetite. While Santy ate his lunch, Danny and I talked about the near explosive political situation in the country, especially the capital of Guatemala City.

"Tim, did you know that life here in the city has become more dangerous almost every day?" he asked.

"No Danny. I had no idea! It's news to me, I didn't know anything about it," I said.

"There's an assassination almost every week here in the capital. It's almost as if the government wants to kill off the brain trust. They're killing doctors and lawyers, people prominent in the city."

"I don't get it. So why are they doing this to their own country?"

"I'm not sure, maybe it's the right wing faction of the government, hard line conservatives. I've been told that these types of murders go on every ten years or so, like they're cleaning house. The guys in power just see it all as a threat to their control, and the money they've accumulated."

"So that's their way of dealing with it? How safe are you and your family?" I asked.

"Man, I know we have to leave this place as much as we don't want to. I think things are only going to get worse and we might have to leave our restaurant to my in-laws and go back to the states," Danny said. All I could do was commiserate with

Danny and the tough situation he was in, pledging my support to him and his delightful family.

Santy ate his fourth slice of pizza and I had two slices that were enough. I just didn't have much of an appetite for lunch. It was all hard to believe that just three years earlier the country was so peaceful! We downed our sodas and with that we finished our lunch. Santy took the two remaining slices *para llevar,* to go, in aluminum foil and a brown bag. This became Santy's first doggy bag. One thing was for sure, Santy had a very good appetite for new foods. We said goodbye for the time being to Danny and then headed back to Zone 7. When we got back to Santy's home, we found his grandmother Doña Victoria waiting eagerly at the door. She took Santy by his little shoulders and buried his face in her loving maternal arms.

"Abuelita, aqui esta dos pidasos de pizza. Son para usted." Santy wanted Doña Victoria to have the two slices of pizza.

"Que sorpresa! Te gusto tu paseo?" She asked if he had a good time.

"Si abulelita, me gusto mucho la pizza," Santy answered her in his cute way of telling Doña Victoria that he very much enjoyed the restaurant and pizza. She hugged him so affectionately and

then released him to enter the *sala*, the living room. He quickly brushed against a young cat that was only half grown and said the words *gato loco,* crazy cat, under his breath, pertaining to his *abuelita's,* cat. Cats were not always welcomed in Guatemalan homes as cats were expected to fend for themselves and find their own food. But it seemed as though Santy's grandmother welcomed the young animal for companionship and took good care of the little cat. We sat and talked a bit, about anything like the weather, about how Santy ate his first pizza. We talked about how the life was in Los Estados Unidos and how her daughter, Miriam, liked America. I told her that Miriam liked decorating our home and how she was *la Raina de la casa,* meaning Miriam was the Queen of the house. With that, Doña Victoria burst out laughing. It was good to see her finally feeling relaxed and happy. She mentioned that Miriam was *mi primer preoccupacion,* her first worry. With that, I said goodbye to Santy and to his grandmother and with the sun setting, found the bus that would take me back to Veronica's home, where I was staying with the Rivera family.

When I got to their home, Veronica's mother, Teco, asked me how everything went at the embassy.

"*Como te fue en la embahada.* How did things go at the embassy? She asked.

"*Pues, por ahora mi cabeza esta nadando con todo que me dijeron.* Well, right about now Teco, my head is swimming with everything they told me at the embassy," I said as I was still dazed and in a state of disbelief, as I told her the embassy people wanted me to go down to Santana, El Salvador to get Santy a visa. It was at this point that Teco told me that the process could end up being nearly endless as well as very expensive.

Teco hatched a plan for me to go back to Asuncion Mita, the part of Guatemala where I served most of my Peace Corps service.

"*Timo, tal ves usted puede ir a Asuncion Mita y pagar para un certificado de nacamiento falsa. Que puede decir que Santy nacio alli y que usted es el papa. Quien va a encontrar que Santy nacio alli o no, o que usted es el papa?* Timo, go to Asuncion Mita where you can possibly get a forged birth certificate that states that Santy was born in Asuncion Mita, Guatemala and that you're his father. Perhaps nobody would ever care to find out where Santy was born, as Asuncion Mita is a five hour drive from the capital of Guatemala," Teco said.

SU MANO EN MI MANO

"Tal vez este plan puede funcionara, quien sabe? Maybe that plan could work, who knows" I said. It seemed certain that this plan could work. I was excited about the idea and began to think that the strategy perhaps had good potential.

I contemplated the situation and began to think that the plan she spoke of might possibly work. And I was willing to take my chances and roll the dice. If I could make this happen, then I'd have to put Asuncion Mita on the map. If there was one place in Guatemala that I could count on then it would have to be Asuncion Mita. Everyone there knew me and had always extended themselves in helping me in nearly any capacity. Maybe, they would be my salvation.

The strategy called for me to go down to Asuncion Mita and then ask my closest friends for some assistance after explaining my dilemma. But before I left the capital I went to Santy's grandmother's home. I told Doña Victoria that I was going to Mita to visit some of the families I knew while on assignment as a Peace Corps Volunteer three years ago. By telling her this, I would avoid any explanation as to my whereabouts for the next week. I didn't want to tell her that I was going to attempt to secure a forged birth certificate, one which would say I was the father of Santy. I thought that if I told her what I was attempting to do she wouldn't trust me and thus prevent me from taking Santy back to Massachusetts. She could become suspicious and confused by my planned deception. After all, Doña Victoria was still on speaking terms with Santy's father, who lived in Guatemala City. If she sensed that I was going to such extreme lengths to take Santy to America, she might renege on her agreement to allow Santy to go live with his mother, Miriam. That was the way life was, so volatile in this part of the world. It was leaving all matters to fate in this fatalistic world where these humble people lived. And I knew very well that if Miriam thought that Santy's leaving would break her mother's heart, then she would be the one to call off the entire expedition. And I definitely didn't want that to happen as I had invested tremendous time and available money to this trip. Doña Victoria had only given her consent to let Santy go to Massachusetts over the telephone. As it was, I already sensed that she was uncertain as to whether she wanted Santy to go to the states. It was that uncertainty that I was trying to calculate. This was my riddle of the Sphinx yet unsolved. I was to later find out that my doubts would be justified but for more simplistic, personal reasons.

The next day I was set to travel to Asuncion Mita, with some cash and all of my traveler's checks on my person as well as my full duffle bag. The buses left for various parts of the country from Zone 4, and from there many people, whether Guatemalan or foreign would come and go and travel to the far reaches of the country. They sometimes went north to the oil rich Petén and Mexico, south to El Salvador, west to the Pacific, called *la costa*, coastal region, or perhaps east to Honduras. In 1979 the Main Bus Terminal was located in Zone 4, well within the midst of the squalor of that part of the city. Other than the dispossessed adults, there were many homeless people whose children went begging for food and money. Among the crowd of good people were those who might rob you when you weren't looking, or pick your pocket if you were not careful. There were small stores, many side walk vendors, beggars, some con artists, young Guatemalan kids shining shoes. Additionally, there were cantinas, cafes, grain shops, restaurants, liquor stores, and gun and ammunition dealers. Many of the humble working class people from the city were traveling to other parts of the country where they might find work. In an agrarian society like Guatemala one lived in either the sunshine or the shadow, either with some fortune or with those down on their luck, barely subsisting. This was a land where the upper class cared nothing about the welfare of the lower class. This was an appalling way to live. No man should be another man's slave. While waiting for my bus, I sat down in a small café to have a cup of coffee and felt a small tug at my shirt. When I turned to see what it was I found myself staring into the eyes of two little children, siblings, a little boy and girl asking for either money or food. Their eyes, while smiling were dark, distinctive, and conveyed their hunger. They both had very short black hair. Most often the heads of very poor children were shaved due to problems with lice and other scalp infections. When they greeted me, they would ask for money and I'd take out all the change in my pocket and hand it over to them; a need that was hard to deny. Sometimes I would buy them some roast chicken with fried potatoes along with two glasses of *leche* or milk.

My departure time had come, as the bus for Mita was leaving at eight in the morning. I boarded the bus and found a comfortable seat. I was lucky to be traveling in one of the newer buses, like the ones that travel over all of the Untied States. Other buses used in Guatemala were very old and worn out, with depleted and burned out shock absorbers. Nevertheless, those old buses continued to be used no matter how uncomfortable, sometimes traveling to the far outreaches of the country. Many of the farmers who came into the city often had their purchased goods stored on the top of the bus. On several occasions, some of the farmers even had young small pigs hogtied with all four feet bound together then placed on top of the bus with the other luggage. This was perhaps a practice that would leave the poor pig very frightened and delirious.

After the driver collected all the tickets, we were headed south on the Pan American Highway for the next five hours. In complete tranquility, one could catch some sleep or sit back and enjoy the ride looking out their window at how the southeast of Guatemala unfurled before their eyes. There was piped in marimba music that played over the speakers, as this was the music of Guatemala. The marimba was a wooden musical instrument originating from Guatemala that looked like a xylophone. The bars on top that made the wonderful dark tones and music were made from rosewood, a hardwood found in the tropical forests of Guatemala. It was usually played by two or three different musicians simultaneously and the music jibed nicely to the ambience of a long bus trip. Often times, a small accordion was played alongside the marimba and the combination of the two instruments created a unique, merry and distinctive sound. Another kind of music played on the buses was ranchero, a Mexican style that included trumpets and guitars. The salsa music played was a very tropical sounding blend of music from Panama and the Caribbean. While the music played, the bus had to climb up on the highway from the city as the Guatemalan capital was set in a very large valley region, built within and surrounded by vast mountain ranges.

Originally, the capital of Guatemala was located in the city of Antigua, just ten miles north of the present day capital. That location was badly damaged by an earthquake back in 1773. To this day, the ruins of that earthquake are a tourist attraction in the city of the very scenic Antigua, set in the path of the volcano, Agua. Since Guatemala City is within a highland mountainous region, the government decided to rebuild the new capital in a very wide and spacious valley called the *Valle de la Ermita.*

With Guatemala City receding far in back of the bus, I sat back in my seat and rested a while. When we finally reached a level plane, I looked toward the right and saw *una finca,* a large ranch where the wealthy owner raised Black Angus beef cattle. The cattle were out in a highly secure and spacious green pasture. These animals were very big and healthy looking, and organically fed and grown as they had the luxury of grazing and eating all day.

The man who owned the ranch raised them so that he would have the beef provided for his family as well as selling the meat locally. It was hard to imagine that these docile, friendly, passive creatures would one day be taken to market. As we traveled on, I could see the people of Guatemala working in their fields either cutting corn or attending to their livestock. The main highway cut through the land and there wasn't much that could be seen while just driving through. However, the towns and small cities were located well beyond the swathing asphalt of the highway. While about two hours into the trip, I happened to see a dead horse on the side of the highway that had been hit and killed by a car, bus or truck. I looked up from my window and saw many vultures circling from above. They always seemed to know when to show up. There were vultures in and around the remains, all eating up the flesh very quickly. They survived by eating up road kill and they did a good job of it too. They were a very homely looking bird but they were a welcome sight as otherwise the carcasses of the large dead animals could have created a health problem. A dead horse or cow was just too big for the people to bury and there wasn't any heavy equipment in the campo to remove them either, other than possibly a pair of oxen and cart.

From a distance I could see the other famous lake of Guatemala called Lake Amatitlan. This lake was about five miles south of the capital. It was not quite as nice as Lake Atitlan but it still attracted a great deal of tourists. Amatitlan is smaller and less spectacular. Steam rises from this warm water lake and medicinal sulfur springs are found along the banks. The nearby volcano Pacaya erupted in 1974 while I was still in training and Pacaya's night time show didn't disappoint. To see red hot molten lava flying in the air at night is very much a wonder of nature. When Pacaya erupted a great deal of calcium and phosphorous was jettisoned into the air via all the smoke. In turn, when the smoke settled onto the land it provided great minerals for the soil. This nourishment helped to provide an excellent source of food and nutrition for the Blank Angus, as well as all other cattle that grazed on the farmlands.

The bus was an express to Jutiapa, a city that was still ten miles away before reaching Asuncion Mita to the south. As we traveled to the *Oriente,* or the dry lowlands, in the southeast of Guatemala, it was easy to see why the people called this part of Guatemala a semi desert region. The flourishing trees of earlier were becoming scarce and the land looked browner instead of tropical green. This was because of the very dry higher temperatures in this part of the country. Nevertheless, when looking at the cornfields it seemed as though the rows of crops went on forever, as they should have due to the recent rainy season. During the siesta time in the middle of the day, at noon, the sun was directly overhead. Being close to the equator, naturally made the climate very hot at times with many people passionately saying *"Que calor,"* It's so hot!

SU MANO EN MI MANO

During this dry season the dust from the unpaved streets further aggravated the living conditions by covering everything with soot.

Finally after reaching Jutiapa, the bus pulled into the terminal and we stopped for fifteen minutes. This junction was of course much smaller than that of Guatemala City.

After getting off the bus to stretch, I could immediately sense the dry heat. It must have been very close to one hundred degrees and the only shade was either back at the bus or the roof of the scruffy looking bus station. There was a feeling of emptiness to the center of this town, due to the noon time siesta. On the other hand, it seemed ripe for adventure, just perhaps at a different time of day. Still there were a few vendors on the sides of the bus station. One young man was doing a good business at a small shack that looked like an oasis in all the desert heat. He was making and selling banana milk shakes, made from fresh banana, cold milk and crushed ice. He had an electric blender and plenty of warm water and soap to clean his utensils. Surrounding the terminal were cantinas, stores and government buildings. I sensed that it wouldn't take long for me to feel the vibes and character of this hot and dusty town that could only get hotter. This was the mood of the people and the atmosphere of the culture, sensations of a lifestyle here in the *"Oriente"*, the southeastern part of Guatemala. This was a lifestyle literally authenticated with a loud bang. This usually took place at the end of a gun barrel from a deadly hand pistol. The noon day heat was climbing on the thermometer and temperatures were rising, something similar to a tropical heat wave. I turned the corner of the terminal to return to the bus and was approached by a tall, thin but muscular young man. He had a light complexion and dark hair, slicked back with a shiny pompadour, a style like the American country western singer, Conway Twitty. He was dressed for the hot weather in a short sleeved shirt with faded dark jeans and expensive looking, polished black shoes. This was a man on a mission. At first I thought he was Guatemalan, but I quickly found out that he was from El Salvador, the capital San Salvador, to be exact. He introduced himself as Mario and reached out to shake my hand. Naturally, I shook his hand and introduced myself. Other than the preliminary small talk, I was to soon find out what his ulterior motive was. He stood there and started his spiel.

"Vamos a San Salvador. Vamos a tomar los frios alli. Vamos, pues!"

'Let's go to San Salvador. Let's drink some cold beer down there. Let's go!" He talked with such a nice smile that showed a bit of gold and silver in his teeth. He was smooth and cool. I could tell that he was probably good at his gifted con game, so convincing with his composure. Other than those qualities, I found him to be kind of sleazy. I have no respect for people who play this con game. I responded politely but told him I wasn't interested. *"Hay, no hombre. Estoy yendo a Asuncion Mita. Tengo muchos amigos alli y no estoy interestada a viajando a San Salvador."*

'No man. I'm going to Asuncion Mita. I have many friends there and I'm not interested in traveling to San Salvador." But Mario kept repeating himself over and over. And I answered him in the same manner. He probably thought I was a tourist and would possibly welcome the company. But I simply wasn't, and I became even more assertive after a buddy of his came to his side. This man was smaller in stature and had on a white undershirt with scruffy tan chinos. One distinctive thing about him was his baseball hat. He didn't say a word and remained nameless while looking at Mario and then at me. He seemed informal while sizing me up and down. These two guys were looking for prey, and in the hunt to rob me if given the chance. It was probable that these two young men were working together to try and scam whoever they could. It may also have been possible that the two were working as travel agents. Who the hell knew? After telling them that I wasn't interested in beer or going to San Salvador for about the fifth time, I turned my back on them and quickly boarded my bus again for Asuncion Mita. They were hapless and I wondered how long people like these two men could continue on as pathetic con artists. While waiting in the bus different children would enter to see if anyone wanted to buy coffee, soda or cornbread and sometimes hard boiled eggs. After just another ten minutes, we then got started up again and were on our way to Mita. While traveling on the Pan American Highway, I couldn't help but remember the only motorcycle accident I had while riding back to Asuncion Mita one afternoon in 1975. It was the rainy season of September and the downpour was heavy. To make matters worse, I wasn't wearing a helmet and there was a heavy fog that had settled in by the end of the afternoon. I was riding down hill at about forty miles an hour, my visibility was poor and I could only see about ten feet ahead of me, even with my headlight on. Suddenly, I saw a herd of horses that had broken out of their corral and were stampeding across the highway. A palomino ran right in front of me and I hit him down the middle. The front tire and fender of my cycle bounced off the horse while I was sent flying forward in the air for about fifteen feet. I landed on the hard asphalt and my left shoulder took much of the impact. While without a helmet on, my head bounced off the highway twice, once on the left temple and then on the top left side of my head, mid-way down. The palomino ran off with the rest of the horses and looked unhurt. I picked myself up and saw that my bike was off to the side of the highway. My left shoulder was in pain, but as I had worn two sweatshirts under my yellow rain jacket, my left arm and shoulder were unscratched. My head hurt and I was a little dizzy but knew fully well what had gone down. What next happened was possibly a miracle that took place in all the rain, fog and confusion. A married couple from Asuncion Mita was driving home from Jutiapa in a red Ford pickup truck, saw and recognized me on the side of the road. They stopped and I seemed to sense my slight amnesia while they helped me put my motorcycle into the back of their truck. For only about five minutes I didn't know where I was. Due to my serious condition, they quickly took me home to Asuncion Mita, right to the front door of where I lived. One of my Guatemalan co-workers, Antonio "Tonyo" Mazariago, quickly heard about what had happened and came to my aid. At that point though, I started to bleed from the cuts sustained on my head. Due to the shock I was in, the bleeding had been held in check until I had calmed down and reached home. After attending to my cuts, Tonyo took me to Dr. Chang's office where the doctor injected a local anesthetic into my scalp. He then put in two stitches on my left temple and three more to the left side of my head, mid-way down. He gave me a shot of painkiller and sent me home and told me to see him in the morning if I had any further complications. When I got home I realized that my left shoulder was dislocated and separated. As I had been given the shot of painkiller, I went to lift my left arm over my head, and then felt the ball joint fall back into my left shoulder socket. Other than that I had a painful, fairly serious concussion that required rest. Within two or three days I was fine and was able to have my motorcycle repaired. I realized I was very fortunate as my concussion could have been much worse. I was very lucky that no other vehicles were coming from the opposite direction. The two sweatshirts as well as a rain parka helped me escape serious road burn to my left arm and shoulder. From that day on I always remembered the ride and the road from Jutiapa to Asuncion Mita. I was also very grateful to the good people who helped me reach safety so quickly. Afterwards I wondered what ever happened to the beautiful palomino that I bumped into. What did he think? How did he feel? If he could talk, what would he say about the accident? Could horses dream while standing asleep? I hoped he only had a few cuts and scratches. At least I was sure that on that night or the morning after, that magnificent horse never ended up as a roadside kill and dinner to a flock of vultures.

SU MANO EN MI MANO

It seemed as though motor cycle accidents were a fact of life among Peace Corps volunteers. Just six months after my accident, two volunteers who lived in the mountainous northwest part of the country had a horrible accident and one of the volunteers was killed. Ken Roberts and Larry Jameson were both riding home after a day out at work with Mayan farmers. As there were no witnesses, nobody saw exactly what happened. However, it was believed that the two were possibly racing down the highway very fast, when they suddenly collided with one another. Ken Roberts hit the asphalt and his body was thrown hundreds of feet from his cycle, mangled with many broken bones and severe concussion despite his helmet. Larry Jameson hit his head along the asphalt so hard that the entire back of his helmet was completely shaved off, along with the back of his skull. It was determined that he died instantly from severe head trauma with his body twisted and contorted, sustaining many broken bones. It was also possible that the two could have been hit by a motorist. These were some of the many dangers when riding motor cycles and just how vulnerable and exposed they left a person. Many Guatemalan men who were experienced motor cycle riders would tell one that a motor cycle *siempre es peligroso,* riding a motor cycle is always dangerous. I'm grateful to have walked away from my accident relatively unhurt and in one piece, unlike my two fellow volunteers. While one young man's body was sent home for burial, the other's was air lifted back to his home in Chicago where he remained in a coma for nearly thirty days. It was all a tragic reminder of how tenuous life can be.

Meanwhile after a half hour and recalling a very dangerous personal experience, we finally pulled into Asuncion Mita. The bus went directly to the center of the town, where I got off and headed over to the appliance store named, *Almacen Centes,* the Centes Family Appliance Center. Three years earlier when I first came to live here, I quickly realized that I was entering another world, stepping into a different kingdom. Mita looked much like it did when I'd lived there, hot and dusty, like a town out of the American wild west, only with cars and not horses. The only thing missing was the tumble weed.

Colors danced as it was an especially bright and festive sunny morning and I saw many people of all ages filling the streets in this hot campo setting. It all looked like the Latino version of a little Mecca, where all different shades of people were living among one another in harmony. There were some mothers waiting in the pharmacy for a prescription to be filled for their growing babies. Many of these mothers would breast feed right in public without any inhibition or embarrassment as breast feeding was an accepted part of their culture. Some very humble, overwhelmed mothers with their children in tow were headed to the central market in order to purchase black beans, and maybe some cheese, coffee, and milk. This was such a painful sight to watch as these families were very poor and barely had any money to buy basic food essentials. I remembered looking at these people and wondering on many occasions if God had forgotten them. With all respect, I never refused them when they asked me for some spare financial offering, a request I could never deny.

Coming up the street where I was going down was a determined young man with his new Stetson hat on, dress shirt and jeans with tan colored boots made for walking. Apparently the boots were also made for following what I guessed to be a very healthy looking four month old pig leading the way at the end of a rope. He most likely wanted to sell the pig to someone who wanted to continue raising the animal until it weighed nearly two hundred pounds. From that weight it would go to market. That was an ideal weight for market as trying to feed a grain fed pig beyond that weight just wasn't cost effective. The cost of feeding a pig that size would diminish any profit.

Adding to the panorama were taxis traveling from Mita and making stops at each small *aldea,* town, all the way down to the border of Guatemala and El Salvador. The taxis were old vintage American cars, Chevy's and Fords, that were used to transport people for just ten cents for a one way trip. The drivers could actually make a living at this trade as there were plenty of stops, to let more people on and off. And the trip would always go down to the border of Salvador and then return to Mita. Sometimes there were so many people in the taxi that there was barely a place to sit. One might possibly have a young child sitting half on and half off one's lap or be squeezed face to face with a mother who had her five kids in tow. That could be a little awkward but everyone usually got to where they were going. The trips ran like clockwork and this sometime cramped operation added to the day's frivolity with plenty of comic relief thrown in. There was one cab driver I knew who fell in love with a local woman who worked for the Centes family as a maid. At first the two absconded to live down near the border for their honeymoon. But after just three days of passionate love, the cabbie decided he didn't want to remain with his bride any longer. He complained that she couldn't make conversation. But what could he expect as his bride came from a very isolated area in the deep campo where there weren't any schools or means of traveling to other parts of the region? The cabbie finally admitted that *"Pues, asi es la vida aqui. No tengo verquensa."* "That's life for us here. I'm not ashamed." It was all a physical attraction. He finally returned to his cabbie business and the young woman asked the Centes family if they would take her back. Of course they did, as three days is nothing in the solitude of this part of the world. She was fortunate and lucky she didn't become pregnant.

Other than philandering in crazy escapades, cab drivers would sometimes make a trip to the capital, a five hour drive. These transactions were private fares and with some consolation the cab drivers could charge a much higher price as the customer was renting out the cab for just himself. All in all, one could make a living as a cab driver, whether working in the campo or the city. Although their pay wasn't as good as a cab driver in the states, they could definitely prosper if they hustled. Within all the surge of humanity, my eyes searched the landscape, darting from left to right and seeing the bright red, yellow, and blue colors, freshly painted on the outside walls of houses, while looking to recognize old friends.

From this mobile kaleidoscope of humanity, I was immediately met by my friend, Otto Centes, the son of Jesus Centes, the owner of the appliance store. I had gotten to know Otto very well when I served as a Peace Corps Volunteer. Otto was very tall for Guatemalan standards, 6'3" in height, weighed about two hundred and twenty pounds, and possessed a raw and powerful strength. He had a reputation in the town as being very loyal to his family.

Legend had it that about ten years earlier, Otto was working in his family cantina along side his mother, Eneida. Three young armed Guatemalan soldiers stopped for *cervesas,* beer, while passing through Asuncion Mita. One of those soldiers demanded another beer and made the mistake of rudely grabbing and hitting the arm of Otto's mother. Otto immediately went over to the soldier, punched and knocked him out and beat on the other two as well, despite the fact that they each had rifles. As the soldiers realized they were disgraced and very embarrassed, they got up and with their tails between their legs, quickly left the town on foot. Otto was treated like a hero and from that day on was known as a man not to be crossed. He was now a local folk hero with a reputation.

As Otto saw me with my duffle bag in hand, he immediately yelled my name and came over to me, shook my hand and embraced me. His father, Don Jesus or Chus as he was known to all, came over to greet me as well, shaking my hand and warmly embracing me. Before I knew it I was surrounded by the whole family with them taking me to the dining room of their home where we had a very emotional and wonderful reunion. I was very flattered and humbled at the way in which they welcomed me after the three year absence. Throughout the buzz of all the excitement, Otto reminded me of the time I helped him with the chickens he was raising in the ICTA Chicken Project we ran. The letters, ICTA stood for Institute of Science Technology for Agriculture. The ICTA Program was the host agricultural agency that worked together with the Peace Corps in Guatemala. Not only was Otto a best friend, he was also one of my people who participated in the project that I started during my service back in 1975. In addition to running the family appliance business, Otto wanted to raise chickens to earn some extra cash. He purchased one hundred Arbor Acre new born chicks from the Purina Company in Guatemala City. The next day I showed him how to vaccinate them against the disease, New Castle, a disease that caused fatal paralysis in the little chicks. He fed them the best chicken feed that was a special grain diet sold by Purina and was able to sell four pound chickens after just forty seven days. His participation was very successful, aside from the fact that some of his chicks got sick from bacteria infecting their digestive system. During that time in 1976, as some of his small chicks were sick and dying, I rode motor cycle to Jutiapa where I purchased a medicine at an agricultural center.

When I got back to Mita, I injected all of Otto's chicks with the antibiotic and they recovered quickly.

Meanwhile, during my festive reunion, Otto and the rest of my friends who considered me *bien querida,* well loved, were very glad to welcome me since they hadn't seen me in nearly three years. Otto soon took me to the large table that was in the dining room and we all had lunch together. First his mother had her *muchacha de la casa,* house servant, bring out a very large bowl of soup. From that point on the young servant girl served the rest of the lunch and we all ate fried fish with rice and black beans, tortillas, *ensalada,* or salad and *limonada,* or lemonade.

At about mid-afternoon, Otto and I approached his father, Don Chus. He was resting in a hammock with his little Pekinese dog, named Paco, in the open air courtyard in the middle of his home. Off to the close left of Don Chus was perched a beautiful white parrot, named Blanca. I approached Don Chus and explained my mission and the considerable difficulty I was having. He consoled me and said that he would help me out in any way. I then asked if he could perhaps help me get a birth certificate for Santy, one that would indicate that he was born in Asuncion Mita, Guatemala and that stated I was his father. For a minute, Don

Chus looked visibly perplexed as the aged lines across his forehead crinkled prominently. Yet he knew that in his part of this world, nearly anything could be arranged, as long as one was willing to pay cash for it.

"Estoy pensando, Timo." I'm thinking, Timo that we have to be careful with just who we ask to do this. I've never been presented with this kind of dilemma." Don Chus said.

"Do you know anybody who we can trust?" I asked.

"I think I might know somebody in the *alcaldia*, the mayor's office over near the plaza in the center of the town, across from the Catholic Church," Don Chus said.

"Do I even at all know him from the years before? Can I trust him? Do you think he could make up the paperwork and say that Santy was born when I lived down here?" I rattled off, asking nervously. I was intent on finding someone who would vow to remain absolutely silent about this matter.

"Maybe, you know him. It's not so much about the trust as Don Emilio is known for being greedy and if he wants, the whole thing might end up costing you a bit of money."

"So that's the man's name, Don Emilio? I don't remember him. I don't think I ever met him."

"*Nos quedamos asi y veremos en la manana.* We'll wait until tomorrow and then see what he says," Don Chus said.

As Don Chus had given me something to think about, I wouldn't know anything until tomorrow when Don Chus had Don Emilio come over to his home. I was confident that he could somehow persuade the town treasurer to take the risk of printing up a forged birth certificate. Who was Don Emilio, anyway? Was he a decent man? How would I know? Did he go home at the end of the day and kick his dog and punch his wife in the face? Might he take the belt from his slacks and strap his wife and children? Was he a womanizer with an *amante,* a girlfriend on the other side of town? Or maybe his wife might be cheating on him. I remembered that Mita sometimes had an air of decadence to it, with many men involved in risqué behavior. It was in Asuncion Mita where I first learned about Guatemala's accepted marital infidelity. It could be like living in a Fellini movie, like *La Dolce Vita.* Men who carried guns were trigger happy. If a sick debilitated dog was suffering, a gunslinger had no problem pulling out his gun at the behest of the owner, and perfecting target practice in between the eyes of the poor animal from close, point blank range. Some of those men while drunk in public would try and provoke an argument, just looking for a gun fight to end violently. This was a part of the world where murders could be covered up. This was a land of extremes, where impoverished, meek people lived to practice their Evangelical religion and killers tossed back shots of tequila happily laughing while maniacally drunk. Don Emilio might possibly be the type of man who would ask me unabashedly if I was working for the FBI. Or yet even ask me if I worked for the CIA. It was apparent that Guatemalans were very aware of the CIA's past involvement in their country's political process. They had first hand knowledge of how the CIA influenced the outcome of the election process in their country. Most of the men who accused me of being in the CIA were drunk from alcohol. But those very same men would seek me out the next evening in the park just to ask for forgiveness for offending me. Now, why would I think that Don Emilio might be that kind of guy? Maybe he even made a pay off to become the town treasurer. One thing I did know was that in Guatemala, one was either wealthy and in the upper class or one was poor and in the lower class. There were very few people of the middle class. How could one pre-judge Don Emilio. I didn't even know him. As for now, I would have to wait until the next day when Don Chus would have Emilio over. Don Chus calmed me by telling me that the only thing I could do was just wait until tomorrow. While Don Chus dozed off in the siesta with his dog Paco at his side and Blanca chirping away from her perch, Otto had to run the family business. I decided to go out on the town and visit the people and my friends who I hadn't seen in three years.

First off, I decided to visit a very good friend named Doña Billia, the woman who owned and managed a *casa de huespas, un pension*, a very hospitable and reputable rooming house where I had been served three meals a day and slept in a single small bedroom. For those accommodations, I paid thirty five dollars a month. I lived there for about one year while I was serving in the Peace Corps. The large and stylish house had an open court yard that had a flower garden in the middle of it. During the rainy season the rain would pour down from the sky, providing water for all the very colorful flowers. Doña Billia was a portly fifty three year old single woman who had never married because her mother, a devout Catholic, never approved of any of her suitors. So it was not only for religious reasons but also the cultural customs that dictated why she ultimately remained a single woman. Many of the town people knew this and felt very bad for Don Billia because she would never be married. Women in Guatemala were expected to marry at a young age and then have children. Facing this stigma, Doña Billia told me that she had given up on the idea of marriage long ago. Her parents were elderly and they lived in the large house, set off from the rest of the guests. During the day, both parents ran a small store at the front of the main door. When I approached the home, Doña Billia was very surprised and happy to see me.

"Don Timoteo, it seems like forever that I haven't seen you," she said as she gave me her version of a bear hug, grasping and hugging me with her great extended arms. Her mom and dad, who were both in their mid seventies stood up to greet me. They all looked the same as when I left Guatemala at the end of 1976. Doña Billia and I started to reminisce about the time when she helped me get all the mice out of the room where I slept. As it was, my room abutted the family store that was at the front of Doña Billia's house. In the store there was a large bureau/bookcase that had been placed in front of the small entrance that had at one time been used by the family before they decided to have the store. As that piece of furniture was not a perfect seal, very small mice could enter through the cracks of that doorway. One particular night when I was falling asleep, I suddenly felt something very furry next to my right ear. I sat up quickly, realizing that it was probably a mouse. Sure enough, I turned my light on and saw that my room had been invaded by about twenty little mice. They were all playing on the floor right in the middle of my room. To tell the truth, it was comical, watching them play. I decided to turn off the light and go back to sleep because I realized they were practically tame and docile. They weren't about to bite me or cause any trouble. I told Doña Billia the next day and she quickly provided me with a different room. She then cleaned and completely sealed off the entire room that was once mine from the store front. Doña Billia and I thought that the entire episode was humorous. After all, the mice were harmless.

I remember also one time when I was staying over night at a friend's house in Mita and encountered fully grown brown rats. In candle light, I happened to wake up in the middle of the night and saw one walking over to a fruit bowl that had ripe bananas in it. This rat looked like he could have torn the fender off of a Mack Truck. So unassuming, he looked at me fearlessly with indifference and didn't appear to be at all alarmed. I could see that he was a male because he had very large testicles under the base of his tail. From there, he held the blueprint for thousands of his offspring. This one single rat could have impregnated many female rats that would give birth to a progeny every 21 days. Rats are so prolific that females can even become pregnant again while still attending to a liter that's only ten days old, thus beginning the life cycle all over again. Rats are found to live very close to the human population because they usually find people to have a very reliable food and water source. Rats live in unsanitary conditions such as the shanty village of the poor in Mita. Those rats probably carried diseases that they spread after contaminating the food and water of people. With the poorer classes living in less than desirable conditions, they stood a higher chance of suffering from the pestilence that this vermin can spread. An eradication program could greatly help to prevent rats from over populating any domestic setting. However, where the situation comes down to every man for himself, it is hard to foresee this very public health problem changing for the better. As it was down in the campo, the rats didn't fear the poor because they were so habituated to the familiar tolerance of those who were poverty-stricken. All I could recommend was to get a nice big cat to patrol the living quarters. However, to the poor, a cat represented another mouth to feed and would be made to look for and kill whatever the cat could find. It was really a question of raising the consciousness and awareness of the people who lived under indigent conditions.

As I still wanted to visit another family who lived close by, Doña Billia and I cheerfully said good night to one another after I promised to visit her again before the end of my trip. With the sun setting upon the skyline, and my expectation met, I easily crossed over two streets, and walked about fifty yards to the house of Carlos Archilla. Once there, I was greeted by Carlos Archilla, a thirty one year old fit and handsome young man who also ran a small store at the front of his home. He called out to his wife, Flory who came over and hugged and kissed me as soon as I entered the small store. As the store owner, Carlos decided to call the establishment *Tienda Flory* after his wife's name, Flory. Flory was a very attractive, sweet and buxom woman who was about twenty five years old. Together both Carlos and Flory had a beautiful and delightful baby girl, Carmella, who was now four years old. She stood behind the counter alongside her mother, Flory. Carlos showed me a little red haired dwarf piglet that he bought for Flory. At the time that he bought the little animal, he was told that it was a piglet destined to weigh about a hundred fifty pounds. But when it never grew after Carlos made the purchase, Flory insisted they fatten it and then serve the piglet for Sunday dinner within a close future date. The little animal looked real cute and it was hard to imagine that it would someday be Sunday dinner. Flory told me not to stress and worry because after they ate the little pig, it would be going to pig heaven. That resolution was not the most assuring consolation. The little pig would soon meet his maker.

Dusk had descended upon Mita and people were headed over to the central park. From there, people could hear ranchero music that was played over the speaker system in the background. The music was romantic and very much like American country western music in sentiment and theme. The lyrics sung were of love lost, love found and of one declaring his love for his girlfriend. The crowd of mostly young men and women would walk in opposite directions in order to check one another out. It was a time for boys to meet girls, to see and be seen, where couples would walk hand in hand and others would greet friends and simply talk. Young children were accompanied by their parents and everyone enjoyed the simple splendor of this night. There was an old weathered looking movie theater right next to the park that showed old movies in Spanish and English for fifty cents. The theater also served as the place where musical talent shows were held. Meanwhile back at *Tienda Flory*, Carlos and I stood outside reminiscing in front of his store, enjoying the fresh night air that came with a gentle darkness. At least the night could bring an end to another day where ugliness and the open wound of poverty would come to rest in the ethereal twilight. Sleep offered a brief respite from that pain. There were many beautiful, radiant stars out that were looking down at Carlos and me, as we gazed back to greet them. This was the universe where worlds beyond number existed. God's silver tapestry was spread across the night sky into a time without end. While we were talking, I looked up at the front wall that I was leaning on and saw a tanned three inch scorpion making his way down the paint. I pointed at it and Carlos trapped it on the wall and showed me a little trick he had learned a couple of years earlier. He took a small stick and quickly disabled the scorpion. He turned it upside down on its back with the belly exposed and facing us. Carlos then placed it against the wall securely and told me to hold the poisonous tail down with the stick he used. Methodically, Carlos was able to extract the glands from the scorpion that produced the poison it injected. What he did almost surgically was amazing and when the sack was removed the scorpion was disarmed and rendered harmless. Carlos turned it right side up and let it crawl up and down his forearm. He asked me if I wanted to hold it and I thought I'd give it a try. The little creature stepped off into the palm of my hand and just wanted the space to walk on. It raised its tail but couldn't strike. Without the poison, the scorpion had been instantly tamed, as if possessed by wonderment.

SU MANO EN MI MANO

When I lived in Asuncion Mita as a Peace Corps volunteer, scorpions were a constant danger. They would hide in anything they could get under, like a roof tile or on your kitchen counter top under a breakfast plate. During my service I followed the work procedure of my host agency, *Instituto de Ciencia Technologia y Agricultura*, Institute of Science Technology and Agriculture, the ICTA Pig Project. I often times had to root out scorpions from our work site. While constructing the pig pens, scorpions were sometimes under the rocks that covered the ground where we built the housing pen. When they stung, the pain was intense and the poison was enough to make an adult nauseous. If an infant was stung, the baby could possibly die. The climate was perfect for scorpions, as it was for tarantulas and black widows. Some of the other Peace Corps volunteers had to deal with tarantulas on a daily basis by spraying their kitchen floors with a very potent and deadly insecticide repellent in the morning before leaving for work. When they'd arrive home in the afternoon, their floors were covered with dead tarantulas. Black widows were so fast one had to sneak up on them before they ran underneath a floor board. Where some people lived in houses with tiled roofs, spraying a room meant bringing out all the scorpions living in the roof tile. Within ten minutes the scorpions were crawling down the walls, looking to clear their heads. But that was useless as the quick acting lethal poison was already attacking their respiratory system and killing them.

As Carlos and I continued to recall our shared past, we remembered and spoke of the time when a neighbor of mine had just been married. She was a very attractive young woman and just twenty years old. She and her husband as well as their respective families were celebrating their wedding reception at her parent's house. Their home was directly across the street from where I was living, not at Doña Billia's house but at a different dwelling on the north side of the town. It was nine o'clock on a hot Saturday night in June of 1975. The father of the bride hired a marimba band to play for the evening and the crowd seemed very happy and enjoying the reception until I heard what I thought was a firecracker going off. From my house, what I actually heard was a gun shot being fired shortly after the reception began. Suddenly I could hear a lot of people yelling hysterically, coming from the father's house. I quickly put on my shoes with my shirt and pants, and ran to the sidewalk on the side of the bride's home. From there I could distinctly hear a painful and tragic voice that was crying and sobbing.

"Papa, papa, te quiero! Papa, papa, te quiero, te quiero! Popi, father, I love you," shouted the bride several times over and over again. She seemed hysterical,

and in a state of shock. I turned to ask one of the guests what had happened.

"*Senor, que me puede decir de lo que paso aqui?* Sir, can you tell me what happened?" I asked.

"*Mira, Mira, ahi esta el papa de la hija. Esta muerto! Vinieron dos soldados que no estaban invitados. Un soldado tomo su fusil y mato el papa, sin razon.* Look over there on the sidewalk. The father of the bride is dead from gunshot. Two soldiers entered the reception uninvited. One of the soldiers took his rifle and killed the father for no reason," said the guest practically in shock. I saw very vividly, the father of the bride had his chest blown away and a great amount of fresh blood on the cement sidewalk. This was such a tragedy for a young bride to deal with.

Practically everyone from the reception was hovering over the dead father of the bride. He had been shot one time from close range. In all the commotion, I asked the people who shot the father and they told me that two Guatemalan army soldiers had attended the reception as uninvited guests. One of the soldiers who was drunk attempted to ask the bride to dance. As this was very inappropriate, the bride's father intervened to reason with the soldier. At that point the second soldier, also intoxicated, took his rifle and deliberately shot the father in the chest from about two feet away, killing the bride's father instantly. The soldiers quickly gathered themselves and ran from the house and disappeared, swallowed down into the hot steamy night, never to be seen again or brought to justice. They were devoured by the darkness as if claimed by a black tide, stretched and spat out by a fearsome omnipotent, unforgiving power. It was as if they walked upon an evil path where they spawned into more and more soldiers with no names, young green clothed soldiers from the campo with serious, deadly guns and rifles with pointed sharp bayonets. They had killed with the cold embrace of hollow, vacant eyes, with voodoo smiles. The two killer soldiers were consumed by anonymity, guarded in secrecy by *El Ejercito,* the military. It was a devil's alliance of illiterate campo soldiers, the fat cat military and an indifferent upper class. They dominated the country in order to forever keep the poor subservient. The soldiers were at the beck and call of the power structure and were sprinkled in the air, like giant granules of corrosive rock salt. Unfortunately, that was the way things happened in Guatemala. The poor had no recourse, and as far as everyone was concerned, the soldiers had vanished into the defiance that reflected all that was wrong about Guatemala. Somehow, somewhere the devil was dancing.

SU MANO EN MI MANO

Carlos told me that the soldiers were protected by the army and were never heard of ever again. He further told me that if someone wanted somebody killed, a soldier would do the hit for as little as a twenty dollar bill. Aside from that gruesome glimpse into horror and death, I could forlornly recount this wedding tragedy, forever etched in memory.

That was enough nostalgia for one night. As it was close to midnight, I turned to Carlos and said good night. We shook hands and embraced as old friends. It was time to return to Otto's home and get a good night sleep as the next day I'd be meeting with Don Emilio. I told Carlos I'd see him again in the next few days. I had merely told Carlos that I was in Guatemala to bring my step-son, Santy, back to the states. I never mentioned all the difficulty I was having with Santy's paperwork.

Don Emilio arrived at ten the next morning and Don Chus had him enter his small private siesta room where he sometimes went to take an afternoon nap in a hammock. This was the day that would define why I decided to come to Asuncion Mita. The time had come to take the first step in securing the birth certificate. It would have been just as well if it had been raining on the moon, with water falling up, and an egg going back into its shell. It didn't matter. It was a day unlike any other in Mita. I felt confident as the three of us sat there and Don Chus did most of the talking. I heard talk about Don Emilio from some of my friends who claimed all he cared about was *pisto,* money. Perhaps the miserly love of money consumed the thought of this man. The more he could put in his pocket, the more he wanted. He was a fairly tall man and also very thin. His raw-boned face and figure cut through the morning air as he swiftly emerged from the hot dusty side street. His face reminded me of a dark Stealth bomber, so very aerodynamically correct. He wore dark clothing with a Stetson to match. Don Chus introduced us to one another and we shook hands.

"Don Emilio, this young man's name is Timoteo and he's trying to take his step-son back to the United States. The problem he has is that the step-son was born in Santana, in Salvador. When he was a week old his mother took him over the Salvadoran and Guatemalan border. So he's been in Guatemala practically all his life, but illegally, without papers. Can you help him at all?" asked Don Chus. Don Emilio wasted no time with his answer:

"Well, the best I can do for him is to print up and sign a false birth certificate. And for that I have to make a hundred dollars. If the authorities in Guatemala City ever find out that I did this I'd lose my title and wouldn't be able to work at the mayor's office ever again. Who knows, I might even be fined heavily for what I've done," said Don Emilio. Don Chus then looked at me and told me what I had to do. I trusted his judgment above all.

"Well Timo, I'd advise you to take your chances and pay Don Emilio the hundred dollars. You don't want to go into Salvador with the civil war going on. Salvador right now is very dangerous to travel in, even for us here. Don Emilio can save you a lot of time and aggravation," said Don Chus. This was the amount I was expecting; one hundred dollars was a significant round number, *cien dollares,* one hundred dollars. Although I felt like bringing him down on the price, I thought that paying for the birth certificate was crucial. Bargaining would be futile.

"Don Chus, if that's what you think then that's what I'll pay. Guess it looks like I'll pay him the hundred. *Es para lo mejor,* it's for the best," I said to him in Spanish.

And that was how the whole transaction took place, in less than fifteen minutes. I paid Don Emilio with cash, as that was non traceable. Don Emilio got up to leave and we shook hands again on our deal. He told me he would get the birth certificate to me by that afternoon and to simply meet him back at the Centes store. He politely, but quickly walked away. There seemed to be something further odd about the man. Perhaps there was no end to what this man would do for money. But that was just a gross generality and hardly fair for me to say. That would be like painting with a broad brush stroke to cover a large unknown area. I was just as much a part of the operation as Don Emilio, maybe even more so. It was my money that greased this wheel. I was the one who would go on to create this near masterpiece of deception. I would be the one to take the fall and full blame if all else failed. But Don Emilio knew that Asuncion Mita was a good five hour drive from Guatemala City and that he would never have to answer to anybody for what he was about to do. At about eleven that morning, Don Emilio returned, walking back briskly with the sharp features out of a sweltering aura of the streets and handed me the birth certificate in a long white envelope, signed, sealed and delivered. In turn I handed him the one hundred dollars, all in very crisp twenty dollar bills. Perhaps I was teaming up with the devil, but at least I didn't feel like I was selling my soul. Where would I be if and when the devil tried to claim my reputation? I would go down fighting. After obtaining the birth certificate, would I have to rely on more trickery and ruse? If I was discovered would I reach out like Lazarus with one arm to live again, to have a second chance at redemption? Who would account for me? The moral objective is that of saving my step-son Santy while sacrificing myself. There will always be people who would say that my journey wasn't worth all the effort and that the motive was wrong. But that's just a judgment and another point of view. However, that opinion doesn't destroy the bravery of what I was attempting to accomplish.

I still believed there was something sinister about Don Emilio, even though I didn't even really know him. As far as getting Santy out of the country, I didn't care if I had to sometimes solicit what seemed like the help of unknown sinister forces. I would immerse myself, descending into a world marked by desire, compulsion, and conscience. Perhaps I was to inhabit the same violent and corrupt forces that had catapulted Guatemala into the land it is today.

I began to think back to all the horrible things that had happened to the poor of Guatemala. I remembered reading that the Central Intelligence Agency covertly overthrew the Arbenz government back in the early 1950's. President Jacobo Arbenz was trying to lead the Guatemalan people by having the American owned United Fruit Company end their partnership and authority in Guatemala. The United Fruit Company was importing all the best fruit and coffee from Guatemala and making sure the produce was sent to the United States. The humble farmers were paid with meager wages and were treated like indentured servants. In this form of democracy, the Guatemalan government could have a slave class with a clear conscience. There was no land sharing or redistribution as was promised in a government decree. This was the land that was owned by wealthy land owners who were ordered to turn over their ownership to the poor. However, the farmers were not allowed to own any property and were practically looked upon as the lowly peasantry. Guatemala and the Arbenz government were headed for socialism, but the US government perceived this Central American government as a Trojan Horse, for the Communists. Therefore the CIA orchestrated a coup and had the Arbenz government overthrown. This action was based on fraudulent recommendations from the United Fruit Company and other Guatemalan military factions hoping to gain power. Perhaps if the US government had stayed out of Guatemala's internal affairs, democracy would have been established. If not for this wrongful intervention, Guatemala could have flourished and been a regional powerhouse of democracy in Central America. Instead, the Eisenhower administration put a stop to what could have been a model of democratic self-fulfillment and destiny. And this all happened at least six years prior to what took place in Cuba with

Fidel Castro in 1960. These are facts that can't be disputed because it's written in Guatemala's and world history. Back at that time in Guatemalan history, the good thing about the truth was that everyone knew what the truth was however long they had lived without it.

No one, including the fraudulent government takeover forgot what the truth was; they just got better at lying. Tragically the same deception goes on in Guatemala to this day. Needless to say I didn't at all like what had happened to the poor of Guatemala back in 1952, despite the government's decree, called 900. As mentioned before, this reform was meant to dispense idle land from wealthy land owners and redistribute the land to poor peasants. But this decree was never permitted. Everyone in Guatemala and the western hemisphere knew that the Mayan Indians had been terribly treated throughout their history. This was the heart of bigotry and genocide. Didn't the upper class realize that no man should be another man's slave? Apparently not. I could never understand why the poor had been treated so, but the racism they suffered was similar to how black Americans were treated in their struggle for civil rights. But the poor of Guatemala had no end game. Drawing upon this parallel of history, I became even more determined in my mission of bringing my stepson to a land where he would live in what was considered a true democracy. I was now fully focused in what I set out to do, and in a way there was no looking or turning back. From that point on it was going to be a disciplined and total organization with sound mind and body.

PART TWO

I now had the birth certificate I needed to start the process of getting Santy out of the country. I thought to myself that at least I was one up on the scoreboard, and had accomplished a very difficult task. What I didn't then realize was that I had only broken the ground on the journey I had just begun.

I took the envelope with the birth certificate and put it securely in my duffle bag. It was the middle of the day and there were still many things to do and people to see before I returned to Guatemala City. While deciding where to go first, I passed the communal sinks where poor women with their children could clean and wash their family clothing and also any cooking utensils. This setting was free of any charge and the water flowed from all the faucets. They only had to buy and use their own soap. Over time, the women seemed to build up their upper arms from all the scrubbing and washing, thus accounting for their broad shoulders. With the noon day sun beating down on me, I thought I'd have a beer at the new restaurant that was built near the center of the town. While sipping a beer at a table I happened to notice a man arguing with his wife over dinner. The waitress brought the man another beer. He guzzled the beer down and he then took the bottle and violently smashed it on the floor. While being angry and explosive, the man seemed to relieve his temper by breaking the beer bottle. Without causing any further disturbance, the waitress got the man another beer and also returned with a dust pan and broom to clean up the broken glass. There was no age limit in regards to being sold alcohol. Consequently, many young men drank in excess and the local Alcoholics Anonymous had a very large membership.

I will never forget the New Year's Day of 1975 when I was on my way early that morning to buy eggs and milk. As I walked up the small hill to reach the local store, I had to literally step over one young man's body after another. It even looked like somebody may have dropped a neutron bomb and killed all these young men without destruction to any property. They had all gotten so drunk that they had passed out right on the sidewalks in the middle of the night. Getting good and drunk on liquor was considered part of the machismo culture. Another sign of the machismo style was that of carrying a handgun. Most of the men I knew didn't even put their gun in a holster. They would simply tuck it under their belt where it could be clearly seen.

The majority of the men who did carry guns only used them in self defense. However, some men took out their guns when they were drunk, waving them in the air and threatening to use it.

Strangely enough, there was such a man, a well known Doctor Menendez who lived and practiced medicine in Asuncion Mita. He had first studied veterinary medicine at San Carlos University, but then decided to study to be a medical doctor and general practitioner for people. He was also an alcoholic and when he became drunk he would start waving a gun in the air. He had even threatened to kill my friend Carlos Archilla, a couple of years before I ever went to live and serve in Guatemala. On one particular occasion, Dr. Menendez treated an older man in the campo and fell in love with the man's daughter who was very beautiful. Being married himself was not enough to stop Dr. Menendez. He began to force himself on her by visiting the young woman at her home in the campo, even though she told him she had a boyfriend, her fiancé. Still undeterred, Dr. Menendez even considered her his *amante*, or mistress and often brought her extravagant presents. Then one day, the woman's boyfriend happened to come by to visit her while Doctor Menendez was there. When he saw the Doctor, he approached him in a threatening manner asking him to cease and desist. However, Dr. Menendez drew his gun out and shot and killed the young man. Dr. Menendez was never tried for the murder because he claimed self defense, asserting that the young man threatened to kill him. The matter was closed and never reached court. Sadly, many of these people like Dr. Menendez ended up killing somebody or being killed by someone else.

Ultimately, Dr. Menendez was in a gun fight where he shot and killed another man who also drew upon him, fatally shooting and killing him. As the story went, they happened to be playing cards at a dance hall where there were a few other people seated drinking beer and listening to the music from the juke box. It was a place where working girls plied their trade and were circulating among the crowd. Dr. Menendez had one of the girls draped over him, kissing and biting his ear, until he accused the other man of cheating at a game of poker. Sensing danger, the bar girl quickly stepped away from what was about to happen. The other man resented being called a cheat and a liar, and then stood up quickly drawing his gun. He shot Menendez in the chest, puncturing his heart while Menendez drew his gun and shot wildly, hitting the other man in the forehead, collapsing dead before he hit the floor. Dr. Menendez tried to rise from his seat but died while his body crumpled and fell back into his chair. The blood of both men merged near the center of the floor, life and visceral essence of enemies joined together in death. It was said to have taken days to finally scour out the stain with a strong lye soap and bleach. So many people had foreseen and maybe even prayed for the day when Dr. Menendez would die this violent death. He was just that evil. Live by violence, die by violence. I learned that whenever in the presence of such people, it was always best to get up and leave without looking back.

It was the middle of the day and there were still many things to do before I returned to Guatemala City. I still hadn't visited Tuical, the small hamlet of a town where I worked with local farmers in developing better livestock, in particular with their hogs and chickens. I especially wanted to visit a good friend, Armando Dukei who I was bringing a present of two dress shirts purchased from Macy's. I remembered that Armando especially liked the variety of clothing sold in the states. I met him when I first worked in the township of Tuical, as a Peace Corps volunteer. Armando knew a great deal about this part of Guatemala, as he had been born in Tuical. He liked to drink *cervesas*, the local beer, especially the *Gallo* brand. He knew where all the small cafes down at the border were and where they sold the best beer and food. We could often get a complete chicken dinner each for about eighty five cents. Of course, we sometimes had to wait for the cook to kill the chicken. Perhaps, this was where the expression, "ringing the neck" of a chicken originated from. This could take place right in front of the people waiting to eat lunch. It reminded me of how people started up an old model T-Ford by cranking up the engine at the front-end of the car. Once this was done to the chicken, the cooks then let the animal fall and flop around for about a minute or two until it was dead. After this, the bird was prepared for lunch.

After arriving in Tuical via a very sweltering and crowded taxi ride, I reached Armando's house. I tucked the box with the two shirts under my left arm and knocked on the door and he answered. At first he stood there and didn't quite know who I was. After all, in this part of the world it wasn't everyday that an American came knocking on your door. But when he suddenly recognized me and realized I'd returned to visit, he was jubilant.

"Hey Armando, it's me, Timo! Don't you recognize me?" I asked.

SU MANO EN MI MANO

"*Hay, no me digas!* Don't tell me, I was just wondering about you the other day!" he said. We embraced; glad to see one another after my long absence. I then presented him with the two Bugle Boy dress shirts and he tried each of them on in front of his brother, Pepe. Armando strutted and further showed them off to his wife, LaLa, a very attractive, tall and humble woman who kept their home immaculate. While heartily thanking me for the gift, he expressed how he loved the fact that they were made in the USA. Armando owned his *milpa*, a small plot of land where he grew corn that he sold locally. He had just returned that morning after being out in the fields working on his crops. While in the Peace Corps working on the ICTA Pork Project, Armando was one of my farmers who participated in the program. He was very enthusiastic throughout, but had six pigs that didn't gain much weight in the first group he raised. Like all the other farmers, Armando raised the *creoles*, the indigenous pig, and native to that part of Guatemala. Sometimes the hybrid pigs, either fattened very well or their growth seemed stunted, depending on genetics. Armando's first group of pigs was disappointing and didn't gain enough weight. However his second group of pigs thrived, earning him a good profit. Armando and my other farmers didn't make a great amount of money when selling their pigs. But the purpose of the project and the idea behind the program was to utilize the technology that was available to them. This meant growing the corn and the soy beans as well as some of the other ingredients contained in the feed that was prepared and given to the hogs. All the vitamins, minerals and proteins needed to complete the diet could be easily purchased inexpensively and locally at an agricultural outlet store, like the one in Jutiapa. Alas, some customs and traditions are hard to relinquish, as some of the farmers complained that the program wasn't profitable enough with a few farmers saying, *no tiene cuenta*, not worth the effort or wasn't profitable. However, in time many of the farmers learned better methods of improving the feed and what breeds could be purchased locally. Many of them decided to raise the "Red Durock" breed of pig that was by far superior to all other breeds. The advantage was that this breed could be fattened and brought to market within just sixty days.

However, the farmers had the age-old problem of all innovations: Many of the farmers did what their father did, and in turn that farmer followed the tradition of what his father had practiced. It seemed like an endless cycle of cultural lag. As time evolved though, the farmers were changing their strategy and perceived the project as a bank, a way to save and invest their money. What it all came down to was good animal husbandry, which meant practicing better reproduction, feeding, and marketing of their livestock. Armando Dukei was one of my farmers who made and pioneered that change and it was so good to see this man willing to modernize his standard of living.

Corn and black beans were two crops that many of the farmers like Armando grew and later sold and lived off of. These crops were the main staple of food that the people depended on. As Armando and I talked he couldn't help reminding me of the time when we went to sell his corn in the town of Ateskatemka, a well known municipality just over the border of Guatemala and El Salvador. I was aware that most everyone was familiar with Lake Ateskatemka, a large body of fresh water bordering the two countries. During the rainy season huge gray clouds would sometimes hover over the lake. The local people often joked that those ominous clouds were in fact the entire Lake Ateskatemka suddenly levitated and floating about a mile up in the sky. On this day though, as the weather was clear and warm, both Armando and his brother Pepe invited me to go along with them in his Nissan truck while they sold some of their *quintales*, or hundred pound bags of white corn. The ride to Ateskatemka took no more than twenty minutes as we drove along dusty roads with sparse vegetation with a few green bushes and coconut trees. We passed huge fields of tomatoes and corn where the farmers were out attending to their crops in the hot afternoon sun.

It was a Sunday afternoon and as we entered the town of Ateskatemka, we saw homes that resembled the ones in Mita that were made from adobe and then painted in very bright pastel colors. The houses were deceptive from the outside. If they looked big, they weren't once one entered. Compared to Asuncion Mita, this town seemed unusually quiet with hardly any people in the streets or the central park that was customary in most towns. Welcome to El Salvador, land of the hot and steamy, land of the tropical ambience; where it was sometimes hotter at night than it was during the day. So much for atheism. There is a hell after all and El Salvador's hot climate bore a sharp similarity to the inferno.

At that point in time, El Salvador was also a land on the verge of great civil unrest and horror; *Esquadron de Muerto,* the horrible death squads, and a military government that chose to instill fear and terror over one of hope. El Salvador was about to implode and the poor were going to suffer unlike any other time in their history from the military dictatorship that governed them. But when I lived in Guatemala, up until 1977, this blood bath still had yet to start. On this occasion when the three of us traveled to Ateskatemka, it was an unusually sizzling afternoon. The humidity was so fierce that it felt like it was raining when it wasn't.

As we proceeded along we came upon two Salvadoran soldiers each dressed in army fatigues with sturdy black military boots. Their outfits made them look like they were ready for the third world war. The soldiers were located at a very slip-shod, and unofficial looking entry station. They wanted each of us to verify where we came from. The first soldier to speak with us stood at the driver's side of the truck. He was a tall thin man in a dark blue army uniform with an emblem arm patch that signified he was a soldier in El Salvador's army. He seemed professional enough while asking us for documentation.

"Where are you all from?" the soldier asked.

"We're from Asuncion Mita, we're all together," said Armando.

"And what about *el chico,* the gringo?" he asked.

"I'm from Los Estados and I have my Guatemalan driver's license," I answered. I quickly passed over my license to the soldier as he stood there at the driver's side waiting.

"O.K., other than your age, name and face, this doesn't tell me who you really are and why you're here," the soldier countered. Armando then blurted out I was a Peace Corps volunteer living and working in Asuncion Mita.

"So where's your passport?" asked the soldier. I paused a moment, thinking the soldier would let me into the town. This was the first time I was asked to produce my passport in El Salvador.

"It's back at my home in Asuncion Mita," I said.

"Well, I'll let it pass this time, but if you come back here again I want to see your passport," the soldier stated.

"*Esta bien,* fine, thank you for letting me enter," I said. All I could think of was to be polite and respectful, even though I could sense certain resentment. Then from the corner of my right eye I saw the other soldier begin to yell at a young, humble looking, campo woman who was seated on the cement curb at the corner of the street where we were stopped. Many of the corner curbs in the semi desert areas stood very high, sometimes about two feet higher than the street. This was for the rainy season when the flooding ran rapidly through the unpaved streets. The gravel kept on wearing away season after season, exposing large rocks and deeper gravel. Meanwhile, the other soldier who had a very full round face with a moustache was short in stature, very stocky, but nevertheless looked like a thug who was powerfully built. The next thing I saw and heard was unlike anything I had ever seen before. This soldier was both visibly angry and shouting at the thin little woman seated on the curb. And from nowhere, up came his right boot that viciously kicked the poor woman, grazing her in the chest and on her chin. She just sat there in shock and remained obedient to the soldier. It was a terrible sight to watch and what was even worse was that we were powerless to stop the very violent abuse. The reason for our hesitation was that the two soldiers were armed to the teeth and had rifles with bayonets. If we tried to intervene we would have been shot and killed. The cold steel of a bayonet through my chest may have meant a quick death, but it was not the way I wanted to die. My heart went out to that woman but there was just nothing we could do to help her. She sat there looking stunned, as she held back her tears. She didn't even get up to try and escape the abuse but sat there obediently minding her master and abuser. The stocky soldier quickly came over to our vehicle and kept muttering, "*no somos humanos?* Aren't we human?" Whatever made him mad enough to kick the woman in the chest still remained a mystery and unknown. Cleared to move on, we continued driving to our destination where Armando sold his corn. On our way back we couldn't help but keep talking about what had happened to that poor little woman.

We were headed back to Tuical. What had happened was very disturbing to witness and we couldn't get there soon enough. It was as if we had briefly been lost in a time warp and had gone back to a later era where some violent customs had never died, where cavemen continued to carry giant clubs to smash over the heads of their women. Some men in Central America were unduly abusive toward their spouses. At one location where I lived in Asuncion Mita, I had a neighbor who told me he would sometimes take the belt from his pants and strap his wife several times if he felt she was disrespectful to him. On one other occasion he physically pushed her, knocking her to the ground. It was hard to imagine how this man could do all that because he seemed to be such a reasonable person. Some men in this part of Guatemala attributed this behavior as part of the machismo mystique. Many men of this region perceived women to be their property and they expected compliance and submission at all times.

Reminding me of that afternoon trip was sobering and disturbing. I recalled on that late afternoon that Armando and Pepe drove me back to Don Chus's home where I thanked them for the ride and told the two brothers to drive safely back to Tuical. Once inside, I greeted the Centes family and soon sat down to eat dinner. The next day I told Otto all about what happened at Ateskatemka, an unforgettable tale.

Now, three years later, Armando and Pepe were once again driving me back to Mita, only this time under more cheerful circumstances. They drove me right to the front door, where they left me off at Don Chus's home. There was a great sense of déjà vous, but with the assurance that all that came before had in fact happened the way it did. Once inside the home, Otto and I began drinking beer into the evening without any reference to the time of day. I saw that it was nearly ten o'clock at night and said good night to all the Centes family and went to my room where I fell asleep as soon as I hit my bed.

When I woke up early the next day, I knew there was only one other person I wanted to see before I went back to Guatemala City and that man was forty six year old Don Ruben Polanco, who also lived in Tuical. Don Ruben was one of my farmers from three years earlier who participated along with Armando in the ICTA Livestock Project. He was a very benevolent and a devout Christian who was a member of the Evangelical church. He looked like a dedicated church minister. He had a noble face with a full head of hair, dark brown with a bit of gray. He was of average height and weight and carried himself with an air of confidence and command. He was married to a woman who was very devout as well and naturally they raised their three children to be the same. His livestock did very well in the program and he earned a good profit after selling them. Like my other farmers, he grew corn that he sold on the market. He was also skilled as a carpenter, another trade he had acquired earlier in life. He was well known and respected in the community of Tuical and Asuncion Mita.

As I approached his home, I could see Don Ruben on the left side of his house sawing wood when I came up in back of him, hoping to surprise him.

"*Hola, que tal hombre,* Don Ruben, how are you?" I asked.

"Timoteo, how are you? *No puedo creerlo!* I can't believe it! I haven't seen you in so long," said Don Ruben.

"Well, as you might know I didn't have much of a chance to say goodbye to everyone I wanted to back then, so that's why I'm here now," I said with a smile.

SU MANO EN MI MANO

"*Pero, Dios Mio, hombre, estas muy galan.* My God, you still look young and you've put on weight," he said.

"Thanks, it's gotta' be that good home cooking *de mi esposa,* of my wife. I'm down here in Guatemala to bring my step-son to Los Estados," I said.

"So you're married and have a stepson! Well that's going to take a bit of work."

"So far, it's been a little difficult, but I'm working on it. How has everything been since I left?" I asked.

"Well, perhaps you may not have heard but just last year I lost my daughter, Lillian, when she died in my arms after being hit by a drunk driver," Don Ruben said.

"I'm so sad to hear about it," I said in complete surprise, trying to console him. I had no knowledge of this tragedy.

"There were four engineers in two small cars who all came speeding up from the ranchero restaurant that's down at the border crossing," he said.

"On yes, I know the place very well," I knew the location. Down at the ranchero at the Guatemala and Salvador border, I could easily imagine how those men got very drunk after a work day out in the field. After all, the *ranchon,* a grand elegant restaurant was built at the border so that people could drink and eat in style on any occasion. There was no limit to how much alcohol a man could be served and there was nobody to shut a man off. The engineers could drive their cars while under the influence of alcohol as there wasn't a law that prohibited such driving. To make matters worse, most people in that part of the world like to drive very fast without regard to any speed limits. These factors turned out to be a reckless foreshadowing. The ride up from the border is mostly a straight way with plenty of highway in front of a driver. There was also a fair amount of jungle on both sides of the road, unlike the populated areas that were dry and steamy hot with very little vegetation. For the most part, if a ride down to the border was downhill, then the return trip was slightly uphill with few houses or any other establishments with people coming and going. With the car windows down and the breeze blowing across their faces, the engineers were euphoric, loose, feeling lusty and macho as all hell. No fear of the *goma,* or hangover with these graduates of San Carlos University. For them, the best thing for a hangover was another bottle of cheap tequila. It could go on for days, non stop with no reason to quit and sober up. The engineers were driving along in their monster death car with the pedal to the metal. For them it was like speeding along with the roar of the crowd and the smell of the Indy Five Hundred. They may have even imagined themselves to be players in their own, private Bruce Lee movie, complete with fists of fury and swords, regardless for the safety of people on foot. While moving at about eighty five miles an hour, obviously they never anticipated what was about to happen. Like a lethal tsunami, they exploded in a deadly wave upon the small religious community of Tuical, the benevolent and gentle province of people I knew very well.

"The first car veered off to the right onto the side of the highway and struck my daughter, killing her instantly. Other people were hit by the car but didn't suffer any severe injury, just my daughter, Lillian. The driver didn't even stop and get out of the car. They all just continued up the Pan Am, afraid of what would have happened if they had stopped. I knew the engineer, Ramon Castillo, who hit and killed my daughter. He fled like a coward to Guatemala City where he could hide out. And there's nothing I could do because there's no justice here in this part of Guatemala. This kind of thing happens all the time to the poor. Because we can't hire a lawyer to help us prosecute, we're left without justice. But at least Castillo never showed his face in this town again. You would think that a man of his education, being an engineer and all, would take responsibility and turn himself in," said Don Ruben as he looked up and practically shed tears over the agony and death of his oldest child. Don Ruben was right, there was no justice for the poor. The Guatemalan government didn't account for the poor as they were masters at exploiting chaos. The government was adept at making people disappear, at hiding people after they went missing until the government agents tortured them to death. It was a custom that had been going on for nearly sixty years, not much longer than the ages of many of the oppressed and powerless Guatemalans I knew.

Don Ruben was very familiar with this condition in Guatemala, and now he suffered on a personal magnitude. I was powerless to help these people other than to report the situation to my government and to the State Department. However, I was also aware that as a Peace Corps volunteer I would have been prohibited from partaking in any foreign government activity. This made sense as we represented the United States and not any political group affiliated with guerilla or subversive activity. Association with this element could get you killed. A Peace Corps volunteer had to adhere to three basic principles. There would be no political involvement, no smoking of marijuana or other use of drugs and a volunteer could not get a woman of the host country pregnant. If a volunteer broke any of these rules, they were immediately expelled from the country and their service terminated in Washington.

Don Ruben continued to make me further aware about the perils that went with living in a less than democratic government.

"Timo, did you know that most of the presidents elected to office here in this country were Guatemalan Army generals?" Don Rueben asked.

"No, I didn't realize any of that before I served here," I said.

"After becoming very wealthy, the presidents leave office at the end of their four years," he said.

"Where do they get the money from?" I asked.

"It all comes from the United States. People here know about the corruption. The army here isn't protecting the people. It's here to enforce what the government wants. They'll put down any student or civil uprising. That's what they're ordered to do."

"But don't most of the soldiers come from poor families in the countryside?" I asked.

"Yes, but they're from the campo where the education and way of life is very poor. They induct as many as they want. And if a recruit tries to escape they're either shot or taken by force.

"Don Rueben, did you serve?" I asked.

"Yes, I served along with some friends years ago," he said.

We talked about how quickly life could change in this part of the world. It even affected both of us personally. We both knew about how Roberto Chang, one of the brothers Chang, had to quickly leave Asuncion Mita and abscond to El Salvador. Although Don Ruben considered Chang a friend, he would never condone what Chang had done. Don Ruben even mentioned how many people considered Chang to be *un lunatico*, a lunatic. Likewise, I knew Chang and benefitted from his generosity. I had purchased lumber from him for the construction of housing for livestock and he only charged me one dollar for the entire amount.

Roberto Chang was one of three brothers born to Chinese immigrants who had settled in Guatemala after World War Two. The other two brothers both became medical doctors, while Roberto became a successful businessman. He owned a large sawmill and a gas station where he had a mechanic working for him. Both businesses prospered, until one day when a customer named Pedro Rojas, disagreed with the bill he was presented for the work done on his car. On that particular occasion, it happened that both Otto Centes and I had driven to the gas station to buy gas. Chang and Rojas began to argue about the amount of money charged and cost of the repairs. Pedro then told Chang, "*Esta Illena con babosades!* You're full of bullshit!" Chang's temper and sanity had sometimes been in question and this was not a remark that was wise to say to this man. Chang immediately pulled his gun from its holster and fired two shots at close range into the chest of Pedro Rojas and then three more into his back as he tried to run away. Pedro died quickly and Chang got into his car and escaped over the border to El Salvador from where he would never be extradited. Everything happened so quickly. My friend Otto and I were completely stunned as we remained at the gas station until Pedro's family arrived. Once his relatives got to the station Otto and I helped lift the dead body onto the back of his brother's truck. We all covered Pedro's body with a white sheet with only his boots showing. I had never witnessed a murder before in my life, surely something I'll never forget. To the very day Don Ruben and I were talking about the murder, Chang had never been brought to justice. Don Ruben knew that *Pues, asi es la vida en Guatemala,* well, this is life in Guatemala. This was the unfortunate side of life for *los pobres,* the poor in this country, and the reason why Don Ruben and so many others like him had turned to their Evangelical religion. This was a faith that gave these people a voice.

"Well Timo, here in Tuical most of us were Catholics at one time. But we became Evangelicals because we could participate more and have our needs met more than with Catholicism. We had one another and we felt some control over our lives. Our religion gave us peace and comfort in our humble lives."

"Don Rueben, I'm very sorry for the tragic loss of your daughter. I know she was *muy guierida,* well loved by all," I said as I extended my hand.

"Thanks Timo. I want you to know that *para todos, aqui esta su corazon y estas dejando un buen amigo aqui,* this is where your heart is, you're leaving a good friend here."

"It's been so good to see you again Don Rueben. I don't know when I'll ever be able to return, but I'll always say I've got un *million de amigos,* a million friends here in Guatemala."

SU MANO EN MI MANO

With the gnarled, brawny hands of a carpenter, Don Ruben shook my hand and we hugged one another in solidarity. I said good bye to him, not at all certain when and if I would ever see him again. Before that day, what I did know was that the loss of his daughter had forever left him in mourning, put a few more crags in his forehead and many more gray hairs in his beautiful mane of hair.

Although tragedy was a frequent and shared occurrence for the people of Tuical, they sometimes enjoyed triumph over the adversity. Before leaving for the capital, I was approached by my friend Armando Duque. He told me that another farmer, Manuel Montero, a farmer who raised pigs, wanted me to take a look at a large sow that just gave birth to twelve healthy piglets. The problem was that the mother sow had somehow developed a fever and infection, and couldn't pass any of her milk to her young litter. When I took a look at her I wasn't at all sure why she was feeling listless and inattentive. This was not the time for her to be sick, as she looked distressed and incapable of lactating and nurturing her little ones. The young piglets continued to get hungrier by the minute. Naturally, I was alarmed at the situation and in turn I told Manuel that I'd go back to Mita and see if I could inquire as to just what his pig might have come down with.

I hoped on the next bus for my village, Mita, and pondered the thought of finding a veterinarian in Asuncion Mita. It turned out that there wasn't a vet in my town but there was an agronomist who had a very good reputation. After finding the right person, Enrique Montanez, I asked him how much the consultation would cost. He told me that the usual rate was fifteen dollars for a visit on site. That sounded very reasonable and I told him that if Manuel could just pay five dollars, I could come up with the remainder of ten dollars. We agreed to this and Enrique got his leather bag with medicine, antibiotics and syringes, and off we went to the province of Tuical on bus, no more than ten minutes away.

It was the end of a Saturday afternoon in the 95 degree heat. When we arrived at Manuel's home, we were invited inside where I introduced the two men to one another. Enrique explained to Manuel the cost of the procedure. Everything was agreed upon and Enrique set about his work. The first thing he did was take the sow's temperature, which turned out to be high, with fever. He then got out a small bottle of penicillin, filled a syringe and injected the medicine into the pig's right hindquarter. That shot was amazing because the sow was cured and able to pass milk in just two hours of time. Manuel was very pleased and thankful and he shook hands with

Enrique and then with me as well. I hadn't revealed to Manuel that I secretly made a pact with the agronomist where I would pay the majority of the cost. It had to be this way, as I knew Manuel couldn't afford the cost of saving the mother pig.

How do you worship a blessed man on Sunday and ignore him for the rest of the week? What does this world mean to people? The realm of possibility is in all of us and if we don't use it, then it will all go to waste. Think of an idea to change the world or maybe just a little piece of it, and then put it into action. This all turned out to be just another day in the Guatemalan paradise.

PART THREE

Bang, went the bus engine returning to Guatemala City. For me it was "back to life and back to reality," as the saying had a certain mystical appeal. And with that I heard the bus driver yell out, "Jutiapa." As from long tradition, the bus made only one stop at Jutiapa before moving on for the nearly five hour trip to the capital. Five to six hours was the ball park estimate, not that anyone here was familiar with "ball park estimate." That phrase was strictly American, but Guatemalans would say *Mas o Menos,* more or less. One never knew when we might be held up by the bandits, a real possibility. The only thing the bandits wanted was your money and other valuables like a gold watch or a diamond ring. One time while returning from Huehuetenango in 1976, a very picturesque city north of Guatemala City, the bus had to make a sudden stop. An older woman thought she was having a heart attack. It turned out to be a false alarm as she was just having a horrific case of acid reflux. She had indigestion complicated from what was better known in these parts as *la goma,* or a hangover. Regrettably, there wasn't a liquor store in sight until we got to the capital. The Guatemalan remedy for "la goma" was another half pint of tequila, the American equivalent to a very strong Bloody Mary. Guatemalans swore that this worked, like spinning the world the other way.

I was leaving Asuncion Mita and I looked back at the place I thought more of as *un pueblo,* a town than what these people called their city. I wondered when I would ever see my friends again in this part of Guatemala.

The bus was climbing the steep area of the highway and it would be like this for some time until we leveled off. Along the way the bus passed numerous rocky creations and terrain on both sides of the highway. I liked to think of them as monuments to time, and pillars to natural history. These cliffs and huge mountainous boulders were the early volcanic formations that characterized this beautiful country. I had been up close to some of these volcanoes. There were three long inactive volcanoes named Atitlan, Toliman and San Pedro, all overlooking the lovely Lake Atitlan. As mentioned before, the volcano Pacaya erupted after my arrival as a Peace Corps Volunteer in Guatemala. In 1974, while training and learning Spanish in the town of Tecpan, north of the capital, the volcano erupted, spewing molten lava into the night air. Watching the fiery explosion from a safe distance was spectacular. This produced several days of cloudiness due to all the soot that filled the atmosphere. Picai and Aqua were just two of the many other special "monuments to time." Just watching the hot lava flow reminded me of how the country evolved. Looking at the scene was like having a ticket to geological history, dreaming and riding within an imaginary time machine.

I saw large iguanas quickly scurrying across the burning highway. They feared people and motor vehicles while racing to the safety of rocky sides of the highway. The pavement probably heated up to easily over a hundred degrees in the hot sun. These iguanas moved quickly even though their feet must have been conditioned to the sizzling asphalt. Over the eons of evolution, these lizards developed a protective thermal cushion on those clawed feet. The iguanas possessed a certain beauty in their ugliness. While regulating their body temperature they can change colors from green, grey and orange. Back in Mita, I remember how iguana meat was sold from door to door by young kids after they had stoned them to death. My friend, Doña

SU MANO EN MI MANO

Billa even served iguana meat for lunch one afternoon. It tasted much like fish most likely due to their aquatic nature and habitat. There were some people who salivated at even the sight of this lizard. Many centuries ago, the early Mayans hunted iguanas and sold them fresh, while hanging them upside down from their tails in the open air market. Eating the meat of this creature that emerged from the primeval eons ago was a one time experience for me. If one looks into the eyes of an iguana, they convey and beg for compassion, one that pleads for mercy. One look at those sorrowful eyes and a person will never eat the meat of this lizard again. Before all the computer graphics that are used today, iguanas were used in science fiction movies as they were easy to manage and evoked a prehistoric look. They are actually related to dinosaurs, but managed to survive where dinosaurs failed to over the past sixty five million years. They rarely bite and are sometimes kept as exotic pets by people who can afford the time to attend to them. It's even become chic to keep iguanas as household pets in Los Estados. Most people don't realize that iguanas have what is called a "third eye". It is not as visible as the two regular eyes and is used only to sense and distinguish light and shadows. This "pseudo" eye is located right above and in between the iguana's two real eyes. Iguanas are captivating creatures and are found all over Central and South America.

There were even a few tarantulas lazily plodding along, looking for any road kill to pick at. The fine hair on their bodies seemed to shine and sparkle while bristling in the hot sun. Their only worry was the squish of a motor vehicle passing through, near and especially, over them. Tarantulas sometimes made their homes in the corn fields. They would typically dig their hole into about a foot of pure topsoil. They'd hide in waiting below until a small bird or a mouse and insects mistakenly crossed over the hole and then caught in the tarantula death hold. These spiders had big appetites to feed. There was one serious problem with tarantulas encountered by my farmers. When plowing their cornfields with their horse and plow, occasionally the horse's hoof would stumble and sink into the tarantula hole. The spider would then bite and inject the skin just above the hoof with murderous killer venom. The flesh above the hoof would become badly infected after a week. As my farmers didn't have any money for a veterinarian, the hoof developed a terrible inflammation and then the death sentence of gangrene. Sadly, either the poor horse died while lying down or was put out of its misery with a gunshot to the head. In this land of the semi-dessert, it was abundantly clear that death was never far away, but around every corner. Killing seemed to drip like rain from the moisture in the air. Death was so remorseless while it often came with a witch's smile, an evil eye, and a poison brew. A walk into the underworld of this land included a blessing and a way to stop the pain and suffering. But I always went back to my insidious query; did God, for some unknown reason forget about these people? I pledged that in this life I would always be there to help the underdog, to help those who suffered an injustice at the hands of a corrupt power. I was to play on and on to this epiphany. After all wasn't this the way John Kennedy, his brother Robert Kennedy and Martin Luther King died so that one day all men, women and children would be free? Even that concept was hard to sell. Life, liberty and happiness had become so complex. In fulfillment, these concepts came before some young idealistic men and women, modern day Buck Roger type entrepreneurs of the 20th century, who would land feet first in the Peace Corps. They would volunteer in tremendous numbers and represent the virtues of democracy with a near religious fervor, devotion and dedication. If that wasn't a black eye in the face of Fidel Castro, then nothing was. They would serve as self-styled humanitarians and philanthropists, enlisting in this government mission that came from Washington DC. The three aforementioned prophets remained an inspiration after being sacrificed like lambs to the slaughter. Is it just fools who think they can change the world? Don't ever listen to those who call you a fool just because you want to extend the glory and the light. The smallest thing can help when passion is alive.

Continuing on, the land seemed to sit up and take notice of the way the bus powered its way up and then down this region of Guatemala. If this land could talk, what could it possibly tell the free world? One possibility would be to suggest the Guatemalan government give back the peasants the land they had been given in the decree of 1954. It was not too late to right the wrongs of that era. The majority of the population was Mestizo, the mixture of Spanish and Mayan Indian descent. It was tragic how even the Mestizo population condescended and looked down upon the Maya Indians. The Mayans were a very peaceful people and were not about to openly complain about this condition, other than through change via the political process. But that land should have been distributed to the Mayan farmers. Naturally as there weren't any United Nation Peace Keepers to make sure the land was properly distributed, the poor never regained any of the land. Maybe the stars weren't aligned in the Central Americans heavens. In Guatemala, when those in power resist the pressure to change, their answer to the problem is planned genocide. Imagine Mayan men, women and children being hacked to death with machetes. The sharpened instrument is such a helpful implement, but a handy killing tool nevertheless.

SU MANO EN MI MANO

While working in the Agricultural Project in Guatemala, I met and worked with a man who served a seven year prison sentence for Manslaughter. He ended up killing another man with his machete. Granted the other man attacked my worker first and my man defended himself. The seven years he served in prison were unfair as the situation was a "kill or be killed" scenario. Judgment can be harsh and at times unfair, unevenly dispensed.

It was nearly twelve noon and the bus finally churned its way to the giant plateau overlooking the city, what many called, "mi linda Guatemala," my beautiful Guatemala, down in the great valley. There was no direct route to the bus terminal. That meant the bus would make endless right and left turns, even passing under a scaled down version of the Paris Eifel Tower, until it made its final roll into the junction in Zone 4. The city looked festive as usual and all the working people were making their way through the hurly-burly momentum and careening movement that made this land of the eternal spring keep spinning.

This part of the city had been hit hard by the earthquake back in February of 1976. There used to be a large hotel that was only three years old that had been destroyed along with many other tall buildings. On that particular night I was staying at a hostel, an inn known to all Americans as the "Sin Nombre," the hotel named "Without Name," in Zone 1 with a dozen other Peace Corps Volunteers. Early in that morning before the quake, I awoke to the sound of many dogs outside in the city, barking continually. The dogs just wouldn't stop their howling. Then suddenly, we were all woken up by very violent shaking that lasted for about thirty seconds. Via the media we were all later told that this earthquake measured seven point five on the Richter scale. We were all jarred from our sleep and could only think of escaping further danger. However, one of my fellow Peace Corps Volunteers was in a state of panic. He kept talking very fast and was visibly in shock with his face perspiring and as white as a bed sheet. After calming him, we all left the building for the fear of an aftershock and huddled at a small city park that was just across the street. It was about 3:30 in the morning and we were among a multitude of other people who were all waiting to re-enter their homes. After about a half hour and feeling the slight chill from the morning air, we went back to the rooming house where we could get barely enough more sleep until dawn.

With the sun up at 6:00 am, we all arose to see first hand all the severe devastation. Entire buildings had crumbled and streets had buckled under the intense pressure on the ground level.

One thing about this quake was that in some places of the city, the earth had opened up and left huge crevices, cracks and fissures. They were dangerous to look at up close because there was no telling where the giant holes ended or how deep they were.

The breaking news was soon reported to the families of all the Peace Corps Volunteers who were safe and not a single volunteer was lost or injured. As it was, over 30,000 people had been killed in the earthquake, nearly a thousand per second. Those especially affected were the poor who lived in adobe homes as these houses had no support. The walls of these homes simply fell on anyone sleeping, crushing them to death. The highlands of Guatemala and the capital were two areas that were hardest hit, reporting many dead and injured. The lowlands were the least affected as that land tends to be much flatter and less exposed to the fault line. Many of the dead bodies in the capital and outlining areas couldn't be properly identified and were being picked at and eaten by many of the feral dogs that were starving during this crisis. Consequently the corpses were stacked up into massive piles and set fire to. I watched as police officers piled the corpses three feet high and then drenched them with gasoline and set them afire. The mass cremation was the only humane way of disposing of the dead in order to avoid any plague.

During all that time of suffering, I quickly returned to Asuncion Mita and then went out on numerous expeditions, bringing food and water to areas hardest hit in my region of Guatemala. I traveled with Carlos Archilla and his brother in law, Pedro whose pick up truck we drove to the city of Jalapa where we distributed water from a fifty gallon drum barrel. Later on in the ensuing days, I traveled on my motor cycle with another volunteer, Ron Wisnowski to Jalapa, again. From our knapsacks we distributed tortillas and beans to the poor who were left homeless by the quake. It was just so hard for us not to shed tears in front of the young children who approached us crying and begging for some of the food.

Upon returning to Guatemala City in the following weeks, one could see signs in business establishments that read *"Estamos en Pie."* Standing in the face of adversity, the people were proudly saying that "We're on our feet." Sitting in my bus seat and recalling the past, I knew my experience was now all a distant memory that had happened three years earlier and I was now on another very personal mission.

SU MANO EN MI MANO

I grabbed my duffle bag and headed to Veronica's home in Zone 5. I was happy, and anxious to tell the family what had taken place in *Asuncion Mita*. It was so nice outside that I decided to walk to Veronica's home. There was plenty of activity going on in the streets surrounding the entire terminal. It was lunch hour, what was called *almuerso* in Spanish. I could easily sense the smoky aroma of fresh corn and roast pork being cooked over small barbeque grills that were set up along the sidewalks. Naturally while holding the food in hand, many of the people were satisfied to eat a freshly grilled corn on the cob. For some of the poor, this would be the only food and meal they might eat in the day, aside from a dish of black beans with tortillas and a cup of coffee. Other vendors were selling fresh brown sugar that had been packed in small boxes from the sugar cane factory. At some of the locations, women were selling chickens "on the hoof," meaning sold while they were still alive. They were either kept for egg laying or taken home and served for dinner. There were leather craftsmen and carpenters who made whatever their customers paid for.

When I arrived at Veronica's home I was greeted by Teco as her mother was resting and Veronica and the other family members were out on the work day.

"Hola, Timo, como te fue en Asuncion Mita, how'd everything go in Asuncion Mita?" Teco asked.

"Well, I'll tell you, I'm so glad I had my friend, Don Chus Centes speak with the treasurer from the Mayor's office. The treasurer drew up a forged copy of the birth certificate. *Estoy bastante relejado,* what a relief," I said.

"I hope everything goes a lot better for you and you get the visa," Teco said.

"That would be the best thing in the world. I gotta' get this all taken care of by the end of this month," I said.

As for now, I only wanted to contemplate my next move. I knew that presenting the fake birth certificate could either go well or be disastrous. The next day I went and got Santy, and we headed for the US Embassy. It was like starting all over again. I only hoped that I didn't have to deal with the same woman as before. She had seen Santy's real birth certificate from Santana, El Salvador when I first showed it to her over two weeks ago. Fortunately, we were approached by a man who I had not seen before. I thought that he would bode well for us as he was American. He was in charge of the office staff, who were attending to the people as they entered the embassy with paperwork. He had a small brass name pin above the top pocket of his suit jacket that read his name and title, "R. Maxwell, Special Envoy." He was a tall, dark and handsome man with a mean disposition. His Spanish speaking ability was poor at best. He seemed irritable and annoyed by the crowd and would very often have one of the staff help him translate. At times a Guatemalan citizen applying for a visa mildly argued with him. He would then have the embassy security see the individual to the door, while abruptly and defiantly yelling in Spanish, "*esta hombre tiene que salir,*" this man has to leave. He didn't have any patience whatsoever. His attitude seemed very different from the others. As Maxwell and I both quickly surmised that each of us was American, we spoke in English. He approached Santy and I, and wanted to know what we wanted. He was not at all polite, and overall seemed to be unprofessional, even to the point of being hostile. He was probably a Central Intelligent Agent who had been assigned to the embassy as an undercover operative with the CIA. His job here at the embassy was considered to be just a "front." This meant that he was to blend in with the rest of the staff and observe and later report to his supervisors.

"Hi, can I help you?" he asked.

"Yes, I have the birth certificate for my son who is right here with me. I've also filled out all the necessary paperwork for his visa as I want to take him to the states," I said.

"Well that's fine, but you now have to take the child to have his blood tested. You also have to have your blood drawn as well. It's standard procedure in situations like this. That means you're gonna' have to take him to our embassy doctor who will verify the results of the blood tests. From that point the ambassador makes his decision," Maxwell said.

"That's fine. I'll get everything done within the next day or two," I said.

"I'm gonna tell you right now, man that kid doesn't at all look like you. So I think you're gonna have a hard time convincing people that he's yours. He looks Guatemalan and you look American. Has he been raised here in Guatemala?" Maxwell asked.

"Yes, he's been living with his grandmother here in the capital. He looks so much like his mother and her side of the family, you should see them," I said nervously. I felt as though the embassy staff was already on to me, or at least this guy Maxwell was. I was afraid something like this could happen. I knew I had to remain calm no matter what. I had to remind myself that Maxwell was just giving his opinion. Hopefully others would see things differently.

From there, I thanked Maxwell and Santy and I left the Embassy. I didn't realize it, but the days were getting shorter and that of course meant it would be getting darker earlier. But it wasn't quite time to put the city to bed. It was just about 4:00 at the end of the afternoon and so I asked Santy if he wanted to eat pizza with pepperoni for his supper. I explained to him that pepperoni was similar to *chorizo,* Spanish for sausage. He gave me an enthusiastic shaking of his head with an up and down, several times and with that we were off to Danny Capone's "Amichi Capone." We got over to the bus stop and waited about two minutes before the bus pulled up. It was the end of the work day for the people of Guatemala and everyone looked eager to get home. As before, there was a great cross section of people, with business men and professionals all in either suits or sport coats and ties. Other men looked as though they were laborers with short sleeve shirts and denims. Their hands looked strong and rough from cement or grease. They probably worked in construction or under the hood of a car, or practically any other hand skilled profession with sky above and mud below. These trades paid better than most of the unskilled jobs and were coveted as a family would be financially more prosperous. Guatemalan men were always looking for a way to be more resourceful. The women on the bus were in dress suits and were perhaps mostly sales ladies, school teachers and other professionals. Some of the younger men and women loved clothes that were in style. Guatemala City prided itself on what was fashionable and therefore followed all the styles, trends and traditions of the United States. Many of the poor in Guatemala hoped to one day go to "Los Estados." But no matter what their employment was, Guatemalans prided themselves on having a job and earning money. Any of the wealthier people were satisfied to remain in Guatemala as they had everything they wanted. They figured, why go to the United States just to be treated like second class citizens? And in a way, they were right.

All the street noise and the roar of the bus engine along with the black smoke coming from the exhaust, making one stop after another, made for a lively ride as we headed to Zone 1. The bus rolled onto 5th avenue and 12th Street, just a block away from Danny Capone's restaurant. We were now in the commercial district of the capital, on Fifth Ave in Guatemala City where all the shoe and clothing stores as well as pharmacies were located. There were also many banks, restaurants and movie theaters. Other very noticeable businesses were hair solons. The women of Guatemala City devotedly followed the latest hair styles. Immune to recession, the beauty shops always did a good business.

There was a tremendous surge of people on both sides of 5th Avenue. It was alive with many young people window shopping or just checking one another out. There were street vendors who peeled oranges and pineapples. Others sold ice cream and yet others were selling salchichas, hot dogs in a roll. Some of the vendors were even selling small red and green parakeets that were caught in the Petén, the jungle region of Guatemala. These petite colorful birds hovered on a large flat piece of cardboard set on the dirty sidewalk. They looked so sad and had their wings clipped to prevent them from flying away. The little parakeets saw their world from the ground up with tall buildings and people surrounding them.

Zone 1 was "El Centro" and it all seemed well organized, energetic and together. It was estimated that there were a million people in Guatemala City and many of these people worked in the hotels and restaurants, all coming from the many far reaches of this urban center.

Santy and I got off the bus and walked down the street to the restaurant and entered the foyer. We were greeted by a waitress as soon as we walked in. She welcomed us with a cheerful "bienvenidos," welcome to Amichi Capone, and then seated us, handing me a menu. Before she could turn away, I told her Santy and I had decided before hand we wanted a large pepperoni pizza with two orange sodas. Danny came out to the dining area and I stood to greet him with a firm handshake.

"Tim, good to see you again, how's everything going with the US Embassy?" he asked.

"Well, I'll tell ya, Danny things are going a little slow but I can't complain because I just got back from Asuncion Mita. I got Santy's birth certificate all straightened out. At least I think I did, anyways," I said.

"Well that's good because while you were gone there was another assassination. The guy they killed was a local official who had ties to the present administration. While the man was leaving a café with some friends, a motorcycle with two men on it pulled up and shot the man dead. Witnesses said that the man on the back of the bike did the shooting and then the two men quickly sped away," Danny said.

"Did they get a description of the two guys?" I asked.

"I think so. But you know how it is. Nobody really wants to come forward with any info. That just goes to show you how tense things are here in the capital."

"Do you think you're safe enough with the family here?"

"I don't think so. But I know when I leave my in-laws will take over the restaurant. At least the restaurant will stay in the family and the business will keep running," Danny said.

"Where will you and your family go from here?" I asked.

"Well, I'm pretty sure we'll go back to live at my parent's home in the states for a while until we get settled," he said.

"So it looks like you're gonna' have to find work close to home, back in maybe the Boston area. You better leave while it's still safe for you," I said.

"That's more certain every day," said Danny.

And with that the timing was right as I saw the waitress bringing our pizza over to the table. Santy was eager to start eating.

"Santy, say pepperoni pizza!" I said enthusiastically.

"Mmm, yummy," Santy said with a brevity of words, while I gave him two slices to start with. I grabbed a slice and started eating while Danny was already attending to other guests. I ate another slice and enjoyed Danny's recipe of the Italian style for pizza while drinking a bit of orange soda.

"*Mas, por favor?* More please?" Santy asked.

"*Seguro*, sure," I said.

Santy liked the pizza and mumbling with his mouth half full comically motioned to me for another slice. On the whole, Santy seemed more and more like a little man of few words. He never said all that much and was definitely a low maintenance kid, even while completing all the steps of going to the United States. He was usually a cool customer, like the day we went to the post office in his neighborhood to apply for his passport. He sat patiently while the staff quickly processed his black and white photo. We had his passport in just two hours after completion of the usual questions. It remained in my possession until our final days in Guatemala. If Santy sometimes had the look of bewilderment, he was in good company as I was right there with him. The majority of other times he was content and enthusiastic. This was particularly so, especially when he eagerly chowed down on new and exotic food.

We finished the pizza and sodas, then paid and tipped the waitress. I said good night to Danny and with an eye to the future, told him I'd be back before leaving for the states. It was dark outside with the street lights on as well as the light from all the stores and restaurants. We stood at the bus stop and managed to get on a very crowded bus that was headed for Zone 7. Things were tough all around and I felt badly, especially for Danny and his family. He and his wife had a very successful restaurant and now just after two years they had to leave the business in order to avoid the violence consuming Guatemala. Meanwhile, I made sure I kept my eyes on Santy, as he was comfortable on the ride home. I could tell that Santy was quickly developing an appetite for spicy American style foods. It was very crowded on the bus and I had to stand while Santy was able to sit next to where I was practically hanging over him. Before I realized it we had arrived to our destination in Zone 7. The bus stopped and Santy and I were following the line of people who were also leaving the bus. Santy was in front of me and I had my hands on his shoulders. When we were going down the stairs of the rear door, Santy jumped off from the top of the steps before I could reach him. The bus door suddenly closed and started to drive away before I was able to get off. I instinctively yelled very loudly the word "stop." The bus driver understood some English and quickly stopped the bus and opened the rear door again. But it seemed as though another person was standing in the way and half asleep. To make matters worse, he had propped and raised one leg to keep from falling down while he napped. When I started to go down the steps, I had to jump over his leg even though I tried to wake him. Meanwhile I thought I had lost Santy for a moment. After I got off I quickly looked for him. He was sitting down on a bus stop bench and waiting for me about twenty yards away. I ran over to him and gave him a big hug out of relief. It was very dark where we got off the bus and I knew that the night time shadows had only intensified my fears.

For some very unexpected reason, Santy had been patiently sitting for a minute or two. My guess was that he was contemplating life and the universe, unlike any other seven year old. He called me Papa, out of formality and asked me some questions.

"Papa, why does a star fall out of the night sky while a bird doesn't?" Santy asked.

"Well, that's because the birds are meant to fly while stars are not," I said.

SU MANO EN MI MANO

"Where does the sun go at night?"

"The sun has to warm and give light and day to the other half of the earth."

"Why does the moon change its shape?" Santy asked.

"It's because the earth sometimes makes a shade that shadows the moon as it circles our planet. And *abuelita*, Doña Victoria likes to look up at night and see her moon that way," I said in jest. For just a seven year old, Santy was inquisitive beyond his years, while to our backs was a gorgeous full moon here in October. It was just "a marvelous night for a moon dance," or so said Van Morrison. Santy left me impressed. The child was a romantic! Where did this sudden burst of curiosity come from? After sitting, catching buses and eating pizza with a child who I thought was very quiet, Santy had suddenly made up for lost time. I decided to sling him over my shoulder and give him a piggy back ride with the assurance that I could feel his two small hands on my shoulders. At least, I knew where he was.

We arrived at Doña Victoria's home where she had been waiting for us. She too was apprehensive about the somber uncertainty and violence that had descended upon Guatemala City. Perhaps she equated Santy's departure with the evil and how it might gobble up her grandson, making him one of the "disappeared." But I assured her not to worry when Santy was with me. Santy approached her and gave her a big hug and said good night to me while going over to the kitchen for a drink of water. I thanked Doña Victoria and told her I would be back tomorrow to take Santy for another routine visit to the US Embassy. Of course once again, I remained secretive and guarded about what was going on with any embassy procedure. "Routine visit," would suffice for any codename of ongoing embassy matters. It was better this way for everyone involved.

However, the next day was anything but routine for me. Santy and I had to go to the San Louie de Marco Hospital located in Zone 1 on the Second Avenue to see a Dr. Baca, who was the head of the hematology department. I was told by Maxwell that Dr. Baca would have complete control over the results of our blood tests. When we arrived that morning we were told by a medical assistant to wait for Dr. Baca in the examination room. The staff expected us as I was sure that the US Embassy advised them that we would be arriving. First we were told that Santy would give a blood sample and I would as well. I remember that this was very uncomfortable for Santy as he didn't like the needle being stuck into the vein of his inner forearm. I didn't like it either but it had to be done. Nevertheless, the nurse took samples from both of us. She recorded on her chart our names and marked each sample separately. We were then told to wait in the large hallway outside. Suddenly, Dr. Baca appeared and he introduced himself to me. He was an older man, maybe in his late sixties, and tall, perhaps over six feet and with a very noble cherubic face and majestic looking white hair swept back. He looked very robust and perhaps weighed a good two hundred and fifty pounds on the scale. He greeted me with a very heartening smile and we shook hands and spoke only in Spanish.

"Hola, que tal senor, como puedo ayudarte? Hello sir, how can I help you?" Dr. Baca asked. I felt relaxed and confident about Dr. Baca and at the spur of the moment, decided to tell him the truth about everything I was trying to do and accomplish.

"Well Doctor Baca, I'm trying to bring my step-son to the United States where his mother, my wife is residing in Massachusetts. The Embassy seems to be giving me a hard time about all this just because Santy was born in El Salvador," I said.

"Really, well how would you like the blood test to come out?" he asked candidly, while still beaming that big ebullient, expressive and engaging smile of his. As Dr. Baca was the director of the hospital, I was surprised when he asked me that question. As if on cue, I then went immediately into my pocket and pulled out a twenty dollar bill and placed it in his right hand. As his hand was already extended, he took the twenty and casually placed it in the right pocket of his white freshly starched hospital jacket. All of this transpired so fast. I couldn't believe it was happening! My words came so quickly I could barely conceal my joy.

"Well, I'd like my blood test to match Santy's blood test so that it looks like I'm his father," I blurted out.

"*No hay ningun problema.* There's no problem," he said. It was all that easy and he guaranteed me that everything would go as I wanted. It would then transpire as he promised and planned. We shook hands on the deal and Dr. Baca excused himself and quickly left down the corridor to continue in his work day seeing patients.

Hallelujah! Finally something turned out to be easy for a change. And it only cost twenty bucks! Santy and I were now free to go and I could breathe a little easier. And all it took was twenty dollars. The officials working for the embassy couldn't complain as Dr. Baca was a trusted, esteemed colleague and a good friend of embassy staff as well. It only cost twenty dollars to make things cool and kosher. I was ecstatic and overjoyed! At last I began to see an end to this fiasco. I took Santy home to Doña Victoria's and never at all told her or my in-laws, neither Tia Marta nor Uncle Oscar what had transpired. Santy in turn was too young to understand or even remember anything that had taken place that day at the San Louie de Marco Hospital. His blood had been drawn for his visa paperwork and I told Doña Victoria that submitting a blood sample was standard procedure for anyone traveling to the United States. I was astounded as this was one of the best things that had happened up to that point.

The next day I quickly got up and headed for Doña Victoria's home. It was about nine in the morning and the bus drove to Zone Seven. I felt as though I was walking on a cloud, ten feet in the air. I knocked on the door of the house and Uncle Oscar answered.

"Buenas Dias, Timoteo, pase adelante, good morning, come in,"* Oscar said. This was odd, as Oscar had never been there to greet me in the morning.

"Gracias, thank you,"* I said. He led me inside where his mother, Doña Victoria was seated along with Tia Marta. Doña Victoria looked distraught

and upset. Oscar sat next to his mother. We all sat together and Oscar spoke first.

"Timo, my mother is very upset about Santy leaving. And I believe that this trip can't happen. Santy will not go to the United States, it's just too stressful for my mother," said Oscar. I was expecting something like this to happen. Nevertheless, what Oscar said had me very upset, as he hadn't considered the financial cost and how hard it had been for me to arrange Santy's departure. However, I didn't want to let my anger show. I kept my emotions to myself and quickly thought of a way through this confrontation. I focused most of my attention on Doña Victoria.

"Doña Victoria, are you sad that Santy is going to the United States?" I asked.

"Yes, I'm afraid for him leaving. I love him so much, my heart will be broken," she said. Meanwhile Santy was seated in between Doña Victoria and Marta. He didn't say anything but kept quiet while sitting.

"My mother will get sick if Santy leaves now," said Marta.

"Yes, Santy can't go. He's not gonna leave," said Oscar. Oscar wasn't making things easier for me before I spoke.

"Well, let's see. I have an idea. Why don't I just take Santy to the United States to have a visit with his mother, Miriam? Then after the holidays, Christmas and the first of the New Year, Santy will return. Miriam can bring him on the plane. She can visit for a while with her mother and the family," I said. Oscar turned to his mother and looked for her approval.

"That's fine. Just as long as you send him back after the holidays," said Doña Victoria.

"I promise you, that's what I'll do," I said while improvising my conversation.

With that said, we all seemed to be in agreement. But in fact, all along I expected something like this to happen. In life, one should expect the unexpected. The scene had played itself out so many times in my mind. Over and over again I considered all the backlog of nasty mental images running loose in the back of my head. I knew very well that Doña Victoria loved Santy very much. I knew she would be saddened to see him leave. But I also knew that Marta's son, three year old Juan Pablo would take Santy's place when Santy left for

Los Estados. Therefore in time, Doña Victoria would overcome her sadness. I realized immediately that I had to take Santy on this very day and not return to his grandmother's home. And that's just about the way it practically all turned out and went down. When our discussion was over, I told the family that I had to take Santy to the US Embassy for another routine visit. That was the last time Doña Victoria ever saw and kissed Santy good bye. Likewise that was the last time Santy ever saw his beloved grandmother, Doña Victoria. I pondered the thought, if only there had been a different way for them to say good bye to one another. I never wanted to take Santy to his mom under these circumstances. But what I came to do, had come to pass. It all ultimately happened.

Instead of going to the embassy, Santy and I took the bus back to Veronica's house in Zone 5. When we arrived I introduced Santy to Teco and Veronica's family. He enjoyed all the attention and basked in the warmth of their affection. Santy smiled and was comfortable for the time being.

I now had to go to the US Embassy and present Maxwell and his staff the results of the paternity test along with Santy's birth certificate. My stomach was in knots and I was nervous, but not visibly so.

SU MANO EN MI MANO

The bus arrived and it seemed to reach the Embassy so quickly. I got off the bus where it always stopped. My heart was pounding as I entered the main entrance. I went to the first counter and was met by a woman who hadn't spoken to me before. I presented her with the birth certificate and the results of the blood tests that were in a sealed envelope. She briefly looked at them and then to my astonishment asked me to enter the office situated behind her, off to the left. I followed her and entered a very spacious office that was meant for the United States Ambassador to Guatemala. There was a small book case and the ambassador's desk, covered with paperwork had numerous chairs placed around it. I immediately thought that I was about to receive the necessary visa for Santy's passport. But I was very wrong. The ambassador entered the office and introduced himself, as Mr. Lawrence Keating. I stood up quickly to shake his hand, to greet him and we exchanged formalities. I could see that he had something urgent on his mind.

"Mr. Flaherty, just what is it that you're trying to do here at the US Embassy?" he asked.

"Well, Sir, I'm trying to bring my son Santos to the United States so that he can live with his mother. I met his mother when I was a Peace Corps Volunteer here in Guatemala back in 1974 up until December of 1976. I served my assignment in the town of Asuncion Mita down in the Oriente," I said. Mr. Keating looked a bit uncomfortable and then reached for paperwork that was in a black folder on his desk. He reached into the file and took hold of two photocopies of information.

"I'd like you to take a look at these documents, Mr. Flaherty," he said with his right arm extended. I took the papers and then read them. God, oh no, crash went the chariots, the piñata finally burst wide open! I'd been discovered! The jig was up. The papers belonged to Santy's mother, and were photocopies of Miriam's documentation when she had applied for her visa back in 1978. On that paperwork I could clearly see that Miriam wrote that Santy was born in Santana, El Salvador in 1972 and not in Asuncion Mita in 1974, as I had claimed.

"But I'm going to reunite him with his mother and I'm going to give him a good home and adopt him," I said desperately. I was at a loss for words. I begged the ambassador to forgive me and told him I didn't want to go to Santana because El Salvador was at war and very dangerous.

"Oh, we're not going to prevent you from taking the boy to the states. We're going to issue you a visa, but as far as his immigration problem is concerned, you're gonna have to see Major Gonzalez down there at the immigration office on 5th Avenue and 22nd Street. He can maybe help you out in terms of the child's legal status and the fine you have to pay Guatemalan officials," he said.

With that Ambassador Keating handed me Santy's visa and said good bye to me. I walked out of the embassy feeling terrible and lost. I'd worked so hard to try and do what seemed like the impossible.

I thought that one feasible solution to this new dilemma would be to ask El Salvador's embassy for some assistance. I knew that the Salvador Embassy was about five city blocks away from the US Embassy. I easily walked the distance and let my head clear for about ten minutes. When I arrived at the Salvador Embassy I didn't realize that it would be so small. After all, El Salvador was only a five hour drive away and perhaps there wasn't the urgency to devote more resources to having a presence in Guatemala. The Salvador Embassy was all in a small one story building. I entered and I spoke first with a secretary and I asked her if I could speak with the ambassador. The office setting was very informal and the pace looked much slower than the US Embassy. Fortunately there was no crowd to deal with and the ambassador wasn't busy. As the ambassador was very fluent in English, we conversed in such. I figured that I had nothing to lose by telling the ambassador that Santy was my step-son. The ambassador was Rodolfo Montoya and he came over to where I was standing and waiting.

"Ambassador Montoya, I'm attempting to bring my stepson to the United States. The US Embassy has given me a visa that allows him into the states. But they won't help me any further because they have it on record that Santy was born in El Salvador. He's now seven years old and Guatemala Immigration wants to fine me over twenty five hundred dollars because he's been in Guatemala all seven yeas of his life without proper documentation. It's not fair," I said.

"Do you have the child's passport?" he asked.

"Yes, I have it right here," I said while I quickly turned to the page with Santy's photo.

"So who's the child's father?" he asked.

"The father lives somewhere here in the capital," I said. But after just one look at Santy's face, the ambassador became somewhat angry and defiant. His persona did a complete about face.

SU MANO EN MI MANO

"I'm going to demand that the father of the boy come directly here to the embassy. I'll have this matter broadcast on local and national television if need be. The father will come forward," he finished. He seemed flustered and indignant. I was glad I didn't bring Santy, there's no telling how this man would have reacted seeing Santy there with me. The ambassador was irrational. What did Santy's father have to do with this matter? Perhaps Montoya acted this way because of his military background. But in character his tactics seemed more Gestapo than anything else. It was the middle of the afternoon and I figured that the best idea at that point would be to simply slip away and leave without offering any further information. The ambassador was too hostile and unpredictable, all puffed up in his chest, making himself look so important. He was just too full of himself while trying to interrogate me.

I went back to Veronica's home and told Teco what had happened and she was in a state of disbelief.

"Now you might as well go down to the immigration office on 5th Avenue and see what last bit of luck you might find there. It's your last resort," she said.

"I guess so, anything's worth a try at this point. Hopefully the US Embassy hasn't warned them about me. Do you mind watching Santy for another day while I go to Zone 1?" I asked.

"Not at all Timo, I'm here to help you in any way," said Teco.

"Thanks Teco, it really means a lot to me. I'll tell Santy that he'll be staying here again tomorrow," I said. Later in the day, Santy and I sat down at the dinner table to have supper with Teco, Veronica and the rest of their family. After supper we watched television with the family. Santy enjoyed the fun and entertainment and it was good to see him laugh again. When I first brought Santy to Veronica's house he didn't want to remain there. I had to tell him that we would be leaving for the states in just another day and there wasn't time to say good bye to Doña Victoria, Oscar and Marta. He understood that we could be leaving quickly and had to be ready to go to the airport. This seemed to sit well with him and also helped him remember that he might return with his mother, Miriam, after the holidays. Once again it was difficult for me to mislead Santy. But I also realized the consolation that he would have a better opportunity in the states. He would attend a good school and learn English. He would one day go to a good college and make decent money. All of this would be his American dream. For now, night had fallen and it was time to turn in as the next day could be crucial.

I got up early the next morning, right around seven, and had a light breakfast and coffee. Santy happily tumbled down from upstairs and I told him he would be staying for the time being with Veronica's family. He was fine with that and was seated at the dinner table having his breakfast when I left the house. I went to the bus stop and grabbed the bus for Zone 1. Per usual the bus was fairly crowded as many people had risen to go to work in the city. I got off the bus at 20th street and 5th avenue. The Guatemalan Immigration building was only one more block down on 4th avenue. There was a small park between 4th and 5th avenues and the 19th and 20th streets, the city had placed benches and fountains at different locations. This park was cool and comfortable to sit in as it was well shaded with many tropical flowers and trees. Often times, lovers would sit at this park just to enjoy one another's company. There were also various food vendors and young Guatemalan kids looking to shine shoes for just twenty five cents.

Each of the four sides of the park was dissected both horizontally and vertically by the respective streets and avenues. In the hot crystal glow of the Guatemalan sun, there was the rambunctious daily activity in this park. There was the early routine of people going to work and some others at mid-day breaking for their lunch while sitting on a park bench. At times there were humble Guatemalan Mayan Indians who sold their striking hand woven blankets from the seat of the many wooden benches. Their main clientele were the tourists traveling through the city, especially the Americans. Bargaining was expected when buying any of the items such as the blankets, ponchos and other clothing. Sometimes the customer was unrelenting in just how low they thought the price should be. However, after living in Guatemala and seeing how hard the Mayans worked, I soon realized that bargaining diminished and failed to recognize their fine-looking craftsmanship. It must have taken a great deal of work to produce such striking fabric and clothing. If the cost of an item was overpriced then bargaining was fine. Otherwise the Mayan seamstress should be paid for the fine quality of the clothing. Meanwhile the mobile crowd was in and out of the park, a small crossroads of civilization and one of tremendous popular movement and attraction.

The immigration office was on 4th Avenue, located in the middle of the block with the other stores on both sides and a very popular restaurant called "Los Pollos." The Major Gonzalez, who the US Embassy recommended I see, had his office on the second floor. In actuality, I never once saw the enigmatic Major but in jest wondered if he wore his uniform every day and insisted people salute him. However, down on the sidewalk in front of the offices were several immigration employees coming and going into the main building. They might have been returning from their lunch at Los Pollos. They were the working class of people who did mainly clerical work as well as all the red tape and paperwork. They were indispensable to the daily running of the immigration office. Without these workers the organization would not operate with any efficiency.

I began to walk up and down the sidewalk, pacing in front of the immigration office. I never went inside the building. The reason why I never went inside the office was because I happened to quickly get the attention of two Guatemalan employees down front on the sidewalk. They noticed that I was restless and asked me what I was trying to pull off. Their names were Felipe and Diego and they gravitated to me like a couple of magnets. Perhaps they knew that I was ripe for the taking or just had honest intuition. They looked like honorable men and I invited both of them to sit and have coffee with me at Los Pollos, in the shadows of their employment. As I was at their mercy, I told them the whole story of what had happened when I took Santy to the US Embassy to apply for his visa. I told them of my trip to

Asuncion Mita and the birth certificate. I mentioned to them that Santy's mother was up in Massachusetts waiting for me to bring her son, Santy to her. Fortunately for me, Felipe and Diego believed me and took my story to heart. Or maybe they knew a fast buck when they saw it. Perhaps either way, they had seen how corrupt the bureaucracy could be. They also could have believed my entire story and simply felt sorry for me. I told them that the Guatemalan immigration wanted over twenty five hundred dollars as a fine for the seven years Santy was in the country illegally. It was at this point that Felipe explained to me the conditions by which he and Diego would help me. Undoubtedly, they both must have realized how desperate I was. I had been through one gauntlet after another and it was nearing the end of the month of October, the time to return to the states. Felipe, a husky looking man, was in a light tan sport coat with a white shirt and a tie with dark slacks and looked very professional. Diego, the other man was thin and fit looking, and more casually dressed with a dark shirt and chinos. Both men were friendly and seemed sincere, willing to help for a price. Felipe, the more dapper of the two finally spoke of the conditions.

"Mira, look, we can put the necessary stamps and documentation in the child's passport, all for say two hundred and fifty dollars," he said.

"Can you do it for anything less, say for two hundred dollars?" I asked.

"No, for two hundred and fifty dollars and nothing less," he said.

"Alright, I can probably have the money by tomorrow. Where can we meet?" I asked anxiously.

"Meet us in the afternoon at four in the café "Los Primos" on the other side of the park. I'm sure you know where it is. And make sure you bring cash, only cash, we only deal in cash" he said. I was not exactly sure where the café "Los Primos" was but I was certain I could find it. With that decided, we all got up and I shook their hands on the deal in agreement. The two men returned to the immigration building to finish their work day. I was free to move in and out of the sunshine and the shadows.

As this amount of cash came as an unexpected expense, I realized that my money was running very low. I now had only a couple of hundred dollars left. My plane ticket was already paid for. But I still had yet to pay for Santy's one way ticket. I needed two hundred and fifty dollars in cash within the next twenty four hours. Now I had to think of how I could get that amount of money. I thought that perhaps Danny Capone could lend me the money and I could pay him back as soon as I could get the money back home.

As I was already in Zone 1, all I had to do was walk down about ten city blocks to where Amichi Capone was located. As it was only noon I decided to walk on the right side of the street as that was shaded from the hot sun. I walked quickly as my mind was racing so fast. All the while I was also meditating to myself. Meditating helped me remain calm and think about a backup plan in case Danny couldn't loan me the money. As October was nearly over I knew that it would take more than a day or two to have my family wire the money down to me from the states. I didn't want to present my identification at a bank in order for them to cash a money order or a bank note. The clock was ticking! Due to this secrecy, I knew fully well that this operation had become clandestine. Finally I arrived at Amichi Capone. I asked one of the waitresses if she could get Danny for me. She went into the kitchen and Danny came out immediately.

"Danny, I have a big problem and was wondering if you could possibly help me?" I asked impulsively, practically barging into the restaurant.

"Sure, if I can possibly help you I will. What's up?" he asked.

"Well, it seems as though the Guatemalan immigration office wants to fine me over twenty five hundred dollars for the amount of time Santy was in the country illegally for the past seven years," I said.

"Is that the only way out of this?" asked Danny.

"Well, I met these two guys, Felipe and Diego who worked in the front office of the immigration building. I swear I must have walked up and down that block at least twenty times until I finally got the attention of a couple of the office employees. They told me that they could put all the necessary stamps in Santy's passport. But, it's gonna cost me two hundred and fifty dollars in cash for them to do that. I don't have that amount of money left and I was wondering if you could loan me the money until I get home?" I asked.

"Sure, I think I could do that. When do you want the money?" he asked.

"Well, they told me to meet them tomorrow at four in the afternoon in the small café named Los Primos. It's right on the side of the park in front of the immigration office," I said.

"I'll get the money together and give it to you tomorrow. When you get back home just give the money to my mom and dad," Danny said.

"That's fine. I'll give your parents the money as soon as I get back. Thanks so much for all of this, Danny," I said.

"Come by in the early morning. I'll have it ready for you," he said.

"That's great Danny. What a relief. I'll see you tomorrow, that's day 29," I said.

That was good news because my money was running very low. Other that that, everything seemed to be moving very fast. I realized that I had to trust and put faith in the two men at the immigration office as they were my only hope of deliverance. They seemed to be honest men, but who knew? Faith was eternal, especially as it was one of the only means left. The situation was tense all around me where emotions came spilling out. The feeling was of promise, one that could be shared with anyone. Time was marching on, regardless of my getting Santy out of the country or not. It was like some of those Saturday afternoon war movies back in the states, where the enemy used the water torture, like the tap, tap, tapping of the endless water drops on my forehead.

SU MANO EN MI MANO

For now I had to be rational in order to survive in this world of uncertainties.

How to deal with the pressure? Tension was setting in that could be remedied with a quick half pint of strong clear liquor, like some of the tequila. Keep strong while the beads of sweat were breaking across the head and face, until the cool breeze made one shiver. For a New York minute, I felt as though I was free floating in space where there were no limits to freedom. Life appeared timeless, like entering another dimension. But the pain of uncertainty was sharp, persistent and non stop. All of my friends in Guatemala who are still alive were rendered as moon-struck visionaries, lucid earth angles while appearing as an apparition. They walked in from the land of the lost, self proclaimed messengers with logical theories, lonely in the now clouded moonlight. One had to wonder, why was the moon here in Guatemala so much bigger than the moon in the states? It was nearly enough to make a grown man sit up and howl in the middle of the night. How could anyone not love this astounding beauty? It looked so big, shiny and wondrous, appearing like one could reach out and touch the white pock marked surface. And from this moonlight my confidants came with smiles, giving me incentive to move on without fear, to continue in the struggle. They were the best people I'd ever known. We all had the same hopes and dreams. One is born into this world to live and die. There was a beginning and an end. Anticipation became the order of the day. This was the way of coping. The first and last thing on my mind was taking Santy to America. The autumnal winds were blowing all the missing pieces of this experience into place. I imagined the Mayan spirits jubilantly thrusting Santy upwards to their heaven. As if body surfing, he could be passed upon those loving palms in wondrous manner with a sacred care. With all this hope floating from within, I went back to find Santy at Veronica's house. Could these be my final days in Guatemala?

Dawn came at 5:30 am in the morning. I couldn't sleep any longer and got up while Santy was still sawing wood. I downed a cup of black coffee and a hard boiled egg served to me by Teco. Breakfast was always light. I was so anxious to get over to Zone 1 and then go to Amichi Capone. Danny had the two-fifty waiting for me. I didn't want to waste anytime with regards to the matter of meeting Felipe and Diego from the immigration office. Finally the bus that transported me from one Zone to another pulled up to the downtown of the city and I hastily got out. I walked quickly to Amichi Capone where I found Danny with his welcoming smile waiting for me.

"Hey, Danny thanks for getting over here earlier than usual," I said.

"No problem. I'm happy to help out. Here's the money, two hundred and fifty dollars. You've come this far, I guess anything's worth a try at this point," said Danny.

"Thanks so much for all you've done Danny. I owe you man, you're a Godsend," I said.

"Sure, just make sure you give the money to my mom and dad when you get home," he said. Danny and I shook on the agreement and we parted in complete confidence.

With that, I left the restaurant and decided to go down to the park in front of the immigration office. I sat down on one of the wooden benches and I leaned back to try and relax. I began to contemplate all that had taken place while watching the water droplets of early morning dew evaporate in the rising Mayan sun.

So little time left, with so much to finish. Do people ever look at a raindrop and wonder what's going on inside that bead of water? It's a clear liquid that's been around since the beginning of time. It's a complicated element that holds an entirely different world. Maybe people can ponder the difference in life. What goes on when you're about to have a near death experience, maybe something like a car crash? Does your whole life quickly flash before you, or do you only brace for the inevitable? Are there flashbacks from your time in the past or are there also foreshadows into your future. There's a loud and violent collision, as you might be smashing through the windshield headfirst. If you are lying on the ground injured and waiting for the ambulance, do all the people who have been a part of your life now assemble anonymously and surround you? They reach out to shield and protect you. They fall into position like the pieces at the end of a story. They may circle you like the symmetry and beauty of a Stonehenge, like pillars keeping stoic watch and time on a life that bares significance at the possible end. Does it matter who's hovering over you in what might be your final moments?

Can't we all imagine somehow saving the person in danger, pulling a victim from a burning house fire, or a swimmer who may have been drowning or making sure a baby doesn't die from crib death? Sure, we don't go out and perform acts of heroism but we think about being the hero and what it would be like to save a life.

Could it be that we're a cosmic experiment that a higher being has created? Beyond the universe and in between the unknown we live to find the nirvana, full of second chances, of hopes and possibilities where we rewrite the ending. Is there a parallel world that we can only imagine and never realize?

Why do we sometimes arrive at a place that we think we've been before but haven't? Maybe life flashes before us in increments, segments and chunks. As time moves forward, can it shift gears and go into reverse and sometimes sideways? The action is like those beads of water as they gather in the early dawn, falling onto the ground as they reflect what's going on in our world.

If I could tell the future, I could predict a snow storm. If I could foresee a death, would I be god-like? The blind man couldn't see until the prophet placed his hand on his face and eyes. So too was the leper cured and the cripple could stand and walk. This was the way of the healer and the messiah. But even the prophets die. Look, there is a light ahead. It's like the words in the song that Dusty Springfield sang where you keep "wishin' and hopin', plannin' and prayin'." I'd like to believe that sometimes out of the worst, comes something good. In essence we are forever like the stars streaking across the night sky that come crashing to the earth, scratching the surface and making our mark. Believing in this inspiration can be a powerful ally, especially when it's one of the few friends you've got left.

The time quickly passed and it became the four o' clock hour. It was time to head over to Los Primos Café. It's funny how the word "primo," came to have a significant meaning. It's the Spanish word for cousin. When I worked in the Peace Corps with my Guatemalan engineers, we often called one another our "Primos del Norte" or our "Primos del Sur." It meant that we were cousins from the north or they were our cousins from the south. It was all done with humor, both affectionately and with respect. Now I was going to a restaurant named Los Primos to carry out a deal.

Filled with anticipation I walked quickly through the park and over to the street that separated me form the café. As I continued on I was also ambivalent with fear, hoping Diego and Felipe wouldn't try to exploit that fear, so central to this mission. I crossed the narrow lane and could see both Diego and Felipe seated at one of the tables. The café was a cheerful little place that served up roast chicken that turned on a rotisserie. The many whole chickens being cooked gave off a wonderful aroma that hit the senses upon entering the café. At this hour of the day, the place was nearly vacant as the owners were preparing for the dinner crowd that ate later in the early evening. Diego and Felipe waved and motioned for me to come over to their table. They were smiling pleasantly, which I took as a good sign. I sat down at the table and couldn't help but notice the striking and very colorful parrot that was peacefully perched at the back of the café. It reminded me of the beautiful bird that Don Chus had back in Mita. There was a cool breeze blowing in through the windows. Felipe and Diego welcomed me, inviting me to sit as we all shook hands. This was the big day. I still didn't know what to expect.

"Bienvenidos, Timo, por favor sienta, welcome and please sit," Felipe said.

"Thanks, I've been waiting for this to happen all day," I said.

"Do you have the cash?" asked Diego.

"Sure, I've got it right here," handing the two hundred and fifty dollars over to Felipe who began to count the bills quickly with his very nimble fingers. Per usual Felipe was impeccably dressed in a light tan suit. Diego was casually but neatly dressed, wearing a button down dress shirt and slacks, perhaps the more comfortable in the warm temperature of the tropics.

"Fine it's all here, two hundred and fifty dollars. And here is the child's passport," said Felipe. He was about to hand me the passport when he started to thumb through it, making sure all was in proper order. While looking at the passport, Felipe stopped abruptly at the page where Santy's black and white photo was. His eyes drifted down to Santy's signature below his picture. Felipe seemed to be amused at something and I didn't quite know what he was about to ask me. I looked at him smiling anxiously, but mystified. With a big smile on his face, Felipe finally broke his silence.

"By the way, did Santy sign his signature here?" He pointed to the hand written name in black ink, Santos Ramirez. The question slightly caught me off guard but I knew how to answer the question quickly while nervously fidgeting in my seat.

"Oh yeah, you know, *su mano en mi mano,* I put his hand in mine when he went to sign his name and together we wrote his signature," I said, uneasily with a smile. At that point Felipe and Diego both burst out laughing. I began laughing too, out of great relief and perhaps my new found camaraderie.

"That's so *chistoso,* so funny," said Felipe. In turn, I smiled and laughed approvingly, making sure that there was no further question about the authenticity and documentation of the passport.

We all stood up together and shook hands on the deal.

The End

ABOUT THE AUTHOR

Tim Flaherty received his bachelor's degree in Psychology and Speech in 1973 from Emerson College in Boston, Massachusetts. In 1974, at the age of 27, he fulfilled a lifelong ambition to serve in the Peace Corp. He was sent to Guatemala where he served as a Peace Corps Volunteer for nearly three years. He learned to speak Spanish after one year and remains fluent in the language to this day.

Upon completing his service, he returned home to Medfield, Massachusetts and was hired as the Spanish speaking job developer for bi-lingual studies at Keefe Vocational High School in Framingham, Massachusetts.

In 1980, Mr. Flaherty was hired by the Commonwealth of Massachusetts and worked as the Spanish speaking case worker at Walpole State Prison in Walpole, Mass. He successfully completed twenty eight years of employment with the state. During those years, he began writing and submitting various articles in newspapers and magazines. His first publication was in 1991 for a corrections magazine called "Corrections Today." That article was a commentary on female drug addiction. From then on he has submitted various and numerous articles of an eclectic quality, with all being accepted for publication. The book *Su Mano en Mi Mano,* Your Hand in My Hand, The Memoirs of a Former Peace Corps Volunteer is his first book, a non-fiction narrative.